C-2135 CAREER EXAMINATION SERIES

This is your
PASSBOOK for...

Surrogate's Court Clerk

Test Preparation Study Guide
Questions & Answers

COPYRIGHT NOTICE

This book is SOLELY intended for, is sold ONLY to, and its use is RESTRICTED to individual, bona fide applicants or candidates who qualify by virtue of having seriously filed applications for appropriate license, certificate, professional and/or promotional advancement, higher school matriculation, scholarship, or other legitimate requirements of education and/or governmental authorities.

This book is NOT intended for use, class instruction, tutoring, training, duplication, copying, reprinting, excerption, or adaptation, etc., by:

1) Other publishers
2) Proprietors and/or Instructors of "Coaching" and/or Preparatory Courses
3) Personnel and/or Training Divisions of commercial, industrial, and governmental organizations
4) Schools, colleges, or universities and/or their departments and staffs, including teachers and other personnel
5) Testing Agencies or Bureaus
6) Study groups which seek by the purchase of a single volume to copy and/or duplicate and/or adapt this material for use by the group as a whole without having purchased individual volumes for each of the members of the group
7) Et al.

Such persons would be in violation of appropriate Federal and State statutes.

PROVISION OF LICENSING AGREEMENTS – Recognized educational, commercial, industrial, and governmental institutions and organizations, and others legitimately engaged in educational pursuits, including training, testing, and measurement activities, may address request for a licensing agreement to the copyright owners, who will determine whether, and under what conditions, including fees and charges, the materials in this book may be used them. In other words, a licensing facility exists for the legitimate use of the material in this book on other than an individual basis. However, it is asseverated and affirmed here that the material in this book CANNOT be used without the receipt of the express permission of such a licensing agreement from the Publishers. Inquiries re licensing should be addressed to the company, attention rights and permissions department.

All rights reserved, including the right of reproduction in whole or in part, in any form or by any means, electronic or mechanical, including photocopying, recording, or by any information storage and retrieval system, without permission in writing from the Publisher.

Copyright © 2024 by
National Learning Corporation

212 Michael Drive, Syosset, NY 11791
(516) 921-8888 • www.passbooks.com
E-mail: info@passbooks.com

PUBLISHED IN THE UNITED STATES OF AMERICA

PASSBOOK® SERIES

THE *PASSBOOK® SERIES* has been created to prepare applicants and candidates for the ultimate academic battlefield – the examination room.

At some time in our lives, each and every one of us may be required to take an examination – for validation, matriculation, admission, qualification, registration, certification, or licensure.

Based on the assumption that every applicant or candidate has met the basic formal educational standards, has taken the required number of courses, and read the necessary texts, the *PASSBOOK® SERIES* furnishes the one special preparation which may assure passing with confidence, instead of failing with insecurity. Examination questions – together with answers – are furnished as the basic vehicle for study so that the mysteries of the examination and its compounding difficulties may be eliminated or diminished by a sure method.

This book is meant to help you pass your examination provided that you qualify and are serious in your objective.

The entire field is reviewed through the huge store of content information which is succinctly presented through a provocative and challenging approach – the question-and-answer method.

A climate of success is established by furnishing the correct answers at the end of each test.

You soon learn to recognize types of questions, forms of questions, and patterns of questioning. You may even begin to anticipate expected outcomes.

You perceive that many questions are repeated or adapted so that you can gain acute insights, which may enable you to score many sure points.

You learn how to confront new questions, or types of questions, and to attack them confidently and work out the correct answers.

You note objectives and emphases, and recognize pitfalls and dangers, so that you may make positive educational adjustments.

Moreover, you are kept fully informed in relation to new concepts, methods, practices, and directions in the field.

You discover that you are actually taking the examination all the time: you are preparing for the examination by "taking" an examination, not by reading extraneous and/or supererogatory textbooks.

In short, this PASSBOOK®, used directedly, should be an important factor in helping you to pass your test.

SURROGATE'S COURT CLERK

DUTIES
Under general supervision, performs duties requiring a considerable degree of independent action in an office of a Surrogate's Court, either as to one or several or all specialties of Surrogate's Court process; answers over-the-counter and telephone inquiries of attorneys and public; makes detailed examination of petitions, account, and schedules presented by fiduciaries for judicial settlement of their accounts; reviews papers submitted by attorneys to determine if a proceeding is ready to be placed upon a motion or a trial calendar; examines or prepares petitions and orders for the appointment of guardians before presentation to the Surrogate for consideration; in counties where there is a large or very large non-judicial Surrogate's Court staff and necessary probate, guardianship, surrogate accounting or other organizational specialization, may act as assistant to the head of a department, or may supervise such speciality process according to court organization; performs related duties as directed.

SCOPE OF THE EXAMINATION
The multiple-choice written test will cover knowledge, skills, and/or abilities in such areas as:
1. Legal terminology, documents and forms related to Surrogate's Court practice and procedure;
2. Surrogate's Court Procedure Act and Estates, Powers and Trust Law;
3. Understanding and interpreting written material; and
4. Preparing written material.

HOW TO TAKE A TEST

I. YOU MUST PASS AN EXAMINATION

A. *WHAT EVERY CANDIDATE SHOULD KNOW*

Examination applicants often ask us for help in preparing for the written test. What can I study in advance? What kinds of questions will be asked? How will the test be given? How will the papers be graded?

As an applicant for a civil service examination, you may be wondering about some of these things. Our purpose here is to suggest effective methods of advance study and to describe civil service examinations.

Your chances for success on this examination can be increased if you know how to prepare. Those "pre-examination jitters" can be reduced if you know what to expect. You can even experience an adventure in good citizenship if you know why civil service exams are given.

B. *WHY ARE CIVIL SERVICE EXAMINATIONS GIVEN?*

Civil service examinations are important to you in two ways. As a citizen, you want public jobs filled by employees who know how to do their work. As a job seeker, you want a fair chance to compete for that job on an equal footing with other candidates. The best-known means of accomplishing this two-fold goal is the competitive examination.

Exams are widely publicized throughout the nation. They may be administered for jobs in federal, state, city, municipal, town or village governments or agencies.

Any citizen may apply, with some limitations, such as the age or residence of applicants. Your experience and education may be reviewed to see whether you meet the requirements for the particular examination. When these requirements exist, they are reasonable and applied consistently to all applicants. Thus, a competitive examination may cause you some uneasiness now, but it is your privilege and safeguard.

C. *HOW ARE CIVIL SERVICE EXAMS DEVELOPED?*

Examinations are carefully written by trained technicians who are specialists in the field known as "psychological measurement," in consultation with recognized authorities in the field of work that the test will cover. These experts recommend the subject matter areas or skills to be tested; only those knowledges or skills important to your success on the job are included. The most reliable books and source materials available are used as references. Together, the experts and technicians judge the difficulty level of the questions.

Test technicians know how to phrase questions so that the problem is clearly stated. Their ethics do not permit "trick" or "catch" questions. Questions may have been tried out on sample groups, or subjected to statistical analysis, to determine their usefulness.

Written tests are often used in combination with performance tests, ratings of training and experience, and oral interviews. All of these measures combine to form the best-known means of finding the right person for the right job.

II. HOW TO PASS THE WRITTEN TEST

A. NATURE OF THE EXAMINATION

To prepare intelligently for civil service examinations, you should know how they differ from school examinations you have taken. In school you were assigned certain definite pages to read or subjects to cover. The examination questions were quite detailed and usually emphasized memory. Civil service exams, on the other hand, try to discover your present ability to perform the duties of a position, plus your potentiality to learn these duties. In other words, a civil service exam attempts to predict how successful you will be. Questions cover such a broad area that they cannot be as minute and detailed as school exam questions.

In the public service similar kinds of work, or positions, are grouped together in one "class." This process is known as *position-classification*. All the positions in a class are paid according to the salary range for that class. One class title covers all of these positions, and they are all tested by the same examination.

B. FOUR BASIC STEPS

1) Study the announcement

How, then, can you know what subjects to study? Our best answer is: "Learn as much as possible about the class of positions for which you've applied." The exam will test the knowledge, skills and abilities needed to do the work.

Your most valuable source of information about the position you want is the official exam announcement. This announcement lists the training and experience qualifications. Check these standards and apply only if you come reasonably close to meeting them.

The brief description of the position in the examination announcement offers some clues to the subjects which will be tested. Think about the job itself. Review the duties in your mind. Can you perform them, or are there some in which you are rusty? Fill in the blank spots in your preparation.

Many jurisdictions preview the written test in the exam announcement by including a section called "Knowledge and Abilities Required," "Scope of the Examination," or some similar heading. Here you will find out specifically what fields will be tested.

2) Review your own background

Once you learn in general what the position is all about, and what you need to know to do the work, ask yourself which subjects you already know fairly well and which need improvement. You may wonder whether to concentrate on improving your strong areas or on building some background in your fields of weakness. When the announcement has specified "some knowledge" or "considerable knowledge," or has used adjectives like "beginning principles of..." or "advanced ... methods," you can get a clue as to the number and difficulty of questions to be asked in any given field. More questions, and hence broader coverage, would be included for those subjects which are more important in the work. Now weigh your strengths and weaknesses against the job requirements and prepare accordingly.

3) Determine the level of the position

Another way to tell how intensively you should prepare is to understand the level of the job for which you are applying. Is it the entering level? In other words, is this the position in which beginners in a field of work are hired? Or is it an intermediate or advanced level? Sometimes this is indicated by such words as "Junior" or "Senior" in the class title. Other jurisdictions use Roman numerals to designate the level – Clerk I, Clerk II, for example. The word "Supervisor" sometimes appears in the title. If the level is not indicated by the title, check the description of duties. Will you be working under very close supervision, or will you have responsibility for independent decisions in this work?

4) Choose appropriate study materials

Now that you know the subjects to be examined and the relative amount of each subject to be covered, you can choose suitable study materials. For beginning level jobs, or even advanced ones, if you have a pronounced weakness in some aspect of your training, read a modern, standard textbook in that field. Be sure it is up to date and has general coverage. Such books are normally available at your library, and the librarian will be glad to help you locate one. For entry-level positions, questions of appropriate difficulty are chosen – neither highly advanced questions, nor those too simple. Such questions require careful thought but not advanced training.

If the position for which you are applying is technical or advanced, you will read more advanced, specialized material. If you are already familiar with the basic principles of your field, elementary textbooks would waste your time. Concentrate on advanced textbooks and technical periodicals. Think through the concepts and review difficult problems in your field.

These are all general sources. You can get more ideas on your own initiative, following these leads. For example, training manuals and publications of the government agency which employs workers in your field can be useful, particularly for technical and professional positions. A letter or visit to the government department involved may result in more specific study suggestions, and certainly will provide you with a more definite idea of the exact nature of the position you are seeking.

III. KINDS OF TESTS

Tests are used for purposes other than measuring knowledge and ability to perform specified duties. For some positions, it is equally important to test ability to make adjustments to new situations or to profit from training. In others, basic mental abilities not dependent on information are essential. Questions which test these things may not appear as pertinent to the duties of the position as those which test for knowledge and information. Yet they are often highly important parts of a fair examination. For very general questions, it is almost impossible to help you direct your study efforts. What we can do is to point out some of the more common of these general abilities needed in public service positions and describe some typical questions.

1) General information

Broad, general information has been found useful for predicting job success in some kinds of work. This is tested in a variety of ways, from vocabulary lists to questions about current events. Basic background in some field of work, such as sociology or economics, may be sampled in a group of questions. Often these are principles which have become familiar to most persons through exposure rather than through formal training. It is difficult to advise you how to study for these questions; being alert to the world around you is our best suggestion.

2) Verbal ability

An example of an ability needed in many positions is verbal or language ability. Verbal ability is, in brief, the ability to use and understand words. Vocabulary and grammar tests are typical measures of this ability. Reading comprehension or paragraph interpretation questions are common in many kinds of civil service tests. You are given a paragraph of written material and asked to find its central meaning.

3) Numerical ability

Number skills can be tested by the familiar arithmetic problem, by checking paired lists of numbers to see which are alike and which are different, or by interpreting charts and graphs. In the latter test, a graph may be printed in the test booklet which you are asked to use as the basis for answering questions.

4) Observation

A popular test for law-enforcement positions is the observation test. A picture is shown to you for several minutes, then taken away. Questions about the picture test your ability to observe both details and larger elements.

5) Following directions

In many positions in the public service, the employee must be able to carry out written instructions dependably and accurately. You may be given a chart with several columns, each column listing a variety of information. The questions require you to carry out directions involving the information given in the chart.

6) Skills and aptitudes

Performance tests effectively measure some manual skills and aptitudes. When the skill is one in which you are trained, such as typing or shorthand, you can practice. These tests are often very much like those given in business school or high school courses. For many of the other skills and aptitudes, however, no short-time preparation can be made. Skills and abilities natural to you or that you have developed throughout your lifetime are being tested.

Many of the general questions just described provide all the data needed to answer the questions and ask you to use your reasoning ability to find the answers. Your best preparation for these tests, as well as for tests of facts and ideas, is to be at your physical and mental best. You, no doubt, have your own methods of getting into an exam-taking mood and keeping "in shape." The next section lists some ideas on this subject.

IV. KINDS OF QUESTIONS

Only rarely is the "essay" question, which you answer in narrative form, used in civil service tests. Civil service tests are usually of the short-answer type. Full instructions for answering these questions will be given to you at the examination. But in case this is your first experience with short-answer questions and separate answer sheets, here is what you need to know:

1) Multiple-choice Questions

Most popular of the short-answer questions is the "multiple choice" or "best answer" question. It can be used, for example, to test for factual knowledge, ability to solve problems or judgment in meeting situations found at work.

A multiple-choice question is normally one of three types—
- It can begin with an incomplete statement followed by several possible endings. You are to find the one ending which *best* completes the statement, although some of the others may not be entirely wrong.
- It can also be a complete statement in the form of a question which is answered by choosing one of the statements listed.

- It can be in the form of a problem – again you select the best answer.

Here is an example of a multiple-choice question with a discussion which should give you some clues as to the method for choosing the right answer:

When an employee has a complaint about his assignment, the action which will *best* help him overcome his difficulty is to
   A. discuss his difficulty with his coworkers
   B. take the problem to the head of the organization
   C. take the problem to the person who gave him the assignment
   D. say nothing to anyone about his complaint

In answering this question, you should study each of the choices to find which is best. Consider choice "A" – Certainly an employee may discuss his complaint with fellow employees, but no change or improvement can result, and the complaint remains unresolved. Choice "B" is a poor choice since the head of the organization probably does not know what assignment you have been given, and taking your problem to him is known as "going over the head" of the supervisor. The supervisor, or person who made the assignment, is the person who can clarify it or correct any injustice. Choice "C" is, therefore, correct. To say nothing, as in choice "D," is unwise. Supervisors have and interest in knowing the problems employees are facing, and the employee is seeking a solution to his problem.

2) True/False Questions

The "true/false" or "right/wrong" form of question is sometimes used. Here a complete statement is given. Your job is to decide whether the statement is right or wrong.

SAMPLE: A roaming cell-phone call to a nearby city costs less than a non-roaming call to a distant city.

This statement is wrong, or false, since roaming calls are more expensive.

This is not a complete list of all possible question forms, although most of the others are variations of these common types. You will always get complete directions for answering questions. Be sure you understand *how* to mark your answers – ask questions until you do.

V. RECORDING YOUR ANSWERS

Computer terminals are used more and more today for many different kinds of exams.

For an examination with very few applicants, you may be told to record your answers in the test booklet itself. Separate answer sheets are much more common. If this separate answer sheet is to be scored by machine – and this is often the case – it is highly important that you mark your answers correctly in order to get credit.

An electronic scoring machine is often used in civil service offices because of the speed with which papers can be scored. Machine-scored answer sheets must be marked with a pencil, which will be given to you. This pencil has a high graphite content which responds to the electronic scoring machine. As a matter of fact, stray dots may register as answers, so do not let your pencil rest on the answer sheet while you are pondering the correct answer. Also, if your pencil lead breaks or is otherwise defective, ask for another.

Since the answer sheet will be dropped in a slot in the scoring machine, be careful not to bend the corners or get the paper crumpled.

The answer sheet normally has five vertical columns of numbers, with 30 numbers to a column. These numbers correspond to the question numbers in your test booklet. After each number, going across the page are four or five pairs of dotted lines. These short dotted lines have small letters or numbers above them. The first two pairs may also have a "T" or "F" above the letters. This indicates that the first two pairs only are to be used if the questions are of the true-false type. If the questions are multiple choice, disregard the "T" and "F" and pay attention only to the small letters or numbers.

Answer your questions in the manner of the sample that follows:

32. The largest city in the United States is
   A. Washington, D.C.
   B. New York City
   C. Chicago
   D. Detroit
   E. San Francisco

1) Choose the answer you think is best. (New York City is the largest, so "B" is correct.)
2) Find the row of dotted lines numbered the same as the question you are answering. (Find row number 32)
3) Find the pair of dotted lines corresponding to the answer. (Find the pair of lines under the mark "B.")
4) Make a solid black mark between the dotted lines.

VI. BEFORE THE TEST

Common sense will help you find procedures to follow to get ready for an examination. Too many of us, however, overlook these sensible measures. Indeed, nervousness and fatigue have been found to be the most serious reasons why applicants fail to do their best on civil service tests. Here is a list of reminders:

- Begin your preparation early – Don't wait until the last minute to go scurrying around for books and materials or to find out what the position is all about.
- Prepare continuously – An hour a night for a week is better than an all-night cram session. This has been definitely established. What is more, a night a week for a month will return better dividends than crowding your study into a shorter period of time.
- Locate the place of the exam – You have been sent a notice telling you when and where to report for the examination. If the location is in a different town or otherwise unfamiliar to you, it would be well to inquire the best route and learn something about the building.
- Relax the night before the test – Allow your mind to rest. Do not study at all that night. Plan some mild recreation or diversion; then go to bed early and get a good night's sleep.
- Get up early enough to make a leisurely trip to the place for the test – This way unforeseen events, traffic snarls, unfamiliar buildings, etc. will not upset you.
- Dress comfortably – A written test is not a fashion show. You will be known by number and not by name, so wear something comfortable.

- Leave excess paraphernalia at home – Shopping bags and odd bundles will get in your way. You need bring only the items mentioned in the official notice you received; usually everything you need is provided. Do not bring reference books to the exam. They will only confuse those last minutes and be taken away from you when in the test room.
- Arrive somewhat ahead of time – If because of transportation schedules you must get there very early, bring a newspaper or magazine to take your mind off yourself while waiting.
- Locate the examination room – When you have found the proper room, you will be directed to the seat or part of the room where you will sit. Sometimes you are given a sheet of instructions to read while you are waiting. Do not fill out any forms until you are told to do so; just read them and be prepared.
- Relax and prepare to listen to the instructions
- If you have any physical problem that may keep you from doing your best, be sure to tell the test administrator. If you are sick or in poor health, you really cannot do your best on the exam. You can come back and take the test some other time.

VII. AT THE TEST

The day of the test is here and you have the test booklet in your hand. The temptation to get going is very strong. Caution! There is more to success than knowing the right answers. You must know how to identify your papers and understand variations in the type of short-answer question used in this particular examination. Follow these suggestions for maximum results from your efforts:

1) Cooperate with the monitor

The test administrator has a duty to create a situation in which you can be as much at ease as possible. He will give instructions, tell you when to begin, check to see that you are marking your answer sheet correctly, and so on. He is not there to guard you, although he will see that your competitors do not take unfair advantage. He wants to help you do your best.

2) Listen to all instructions

Don't jump the gun! Wait until you understand all directions. In most civil service tests you get more time than you need to answer the questions. So don't be in a hurry. Read each word of instructions until you clearly understand the meaning. Study the examples, listen to all announcements and follow directions. Ask questions if you do not understand what to do.

3) Identify your papers

Civil service exams are usually identified by number only. You will be assigned a number; you must not put your name on your test papers. Be sure to copy your number correctly. Since more than one exam may be given, copy your exact examination title.

4) Plan your time

Unless you are told that a test is a "speed" or "rate of work" test, speed itself is usually not important. Time enough to answer all the questions will be provided, but this does not mean that you have all day. An overall time limit has been set. Divide the total time (in minutes) by the number of questions to determine the approximate time you have for each question.

5) Do not linger over difficult questions

If you come across a difficult question, mark it with a paper clip (useful to have along) and come back to it when you have been through the booklet. One caution if you do this – be sure to skip a number on your answer sheet as well. Check often to be sure that you have not lost your place and that you are marking in the row numbered the same as the question you are answering.

6) Read the questions

Be sure you know what the question asks! Many capable people are unsuccessful because they failed to *read* the questions correctly.

7) Answer all questions

Unless you have been instructed that a penalty will be deducted for incorrect answers, it is better to guess than to omit a question.

8) Speed tests

It is often better NOT to guess on speed tests. It has been found that on timed tests people are tempted to spend the last few seconds before time is called in marking answers at random – without even reading them – in the hope of picking up a few extra points. To discourage this practice, the instructions may warn you that your score will be "corrected" for guessing. That is, a penalty will be applied. The incorrect answers will be deducted from the correct ones, or some other penalty formula will be used.

9) Review your answers

If you finish before time is called, go back to the questions you guessed or omitted to give them further thought. Review other answers if you have time.

10) Return your test materials

If you are ready to leave before others have finished or time is called, take ALL your materials to the monitor and leave quietly. Never take any test material with you. The monitor can discover whose papers are not complete, and taking a test booklet may be grounds for disqualification.

VIII. EXAMINATION TECHNIQUES

1) Read the general instructions carefully. These are usually printed on the first page of the exam booklet. As a rule, these instructions refer to the timing of the examination; the fact that you should not start work until the signal and must stop work at a signal, etc. If there are any *special* instructions, such as a choice of questions to be answered, make sure that you note this instruction carefully.

2) When you are ready to start work on the examination, that is as soon as the signal has been given, read the instructions to each question booklet, underline any key words or phrases, such as *least, best, outline, describe* and the like. In this way you will tend to answer as requested rather than discover on reviewing your paper that you *listed without describing*, that you selected the *worst* choice rather than the *best* choice, etc.

3) If the examination is of the objective or multiple-choice type – that is, each question will also give a series of possible answers: A, B, C or D, and you are called upon to select the best answer and write the letter next to that answer on your answer paper – it is advisable to start answering each question in turn. There may be anywhere from 50 to 100 such questions in the three or four hours allotted and you can see how much time would be taken if you read through all the questions before beginning to answer any. Furthermore, if you come across a question or group of questions which you know would be difficult to answer, it would undoubtedly affect your handling of all the other questions.

4) If the examination is of the essay type and contains but a few questions, it is a moot point as to whether you should read all the questions before starting to answer any one. Of course, if you are given a choice – say five out of seven and the like – then it is essential to read all the questions so you can eliminate the two that are most difficult. If, however, you are asked to answer all the questions, there may be danger in trying to answer the easiest one first because you may find that you will spend too much time on it. The best technique is to answer the first question, then proceed to the second, etc.

5) Time your answers. Before the exam begins, write down the time it started, then add the time allowed for the examination and write down the time it must be completed, then divide the time available somewhat as follows:
   - If 3-1/2 hours are allowed, that would be 210 minutes. If you have 80 objective-type questions, that would be an average of 2-1/2 minutes per question. Allow yourself no more than 2 minutes per question, or a total of 160 minutes, which will permit about 50 minutes to review.
   - If for the time allotment of 210 minutes there are 7 essay questions to answer, that would average about 30 minutes a question. Give yourself only 25 minutes per question so that you have about 35 minutes to review.

6) The most important instruction is to *read each question* and make sure you know what is wanted. The second most important instruction is to *time yourself properly* so that you answer every question. The third most important instruction is to *answer every question*. Guess if you have to but include something for each question. Remember that you will receive no credit for a blank and will probably receive some credit if you write something in answer to an essay question. If you guess a letter – say "B" for a multiple-choice question – you may have guessed right. If you leave a blank as an answer to a multiple-choice question, the examiners may respect your feelings but it will not add a point to your score. Some exams may penalize you for wrong answers, so in such cases *only*, you may not want to guess unless you have some basis for your answer.

7) Suggestions
   a. Objective-type questions
      1. Examine the question booklet for proper sequence of pages and questions
      2. Read all instructions carefully
      3. Skip any question which seems too difficult; return to it after all other questions have been answered
      4. Apportion your time properly; do not spend too much time on any single question or group of questions

5. Note and underline key words – *all, most, fewest, least, best, worst, same, opposite,* etc.
6. Pay particular attention to negatives
7. Note unusual option, e.g., unduly long, short, complex, different or similar in content to the body of the question
8. Observe the use of "hedging" words – *probably, may, most likely,* etc.
9. Make sure that your answer is put next to the same number as the question
10. Do not second-guess unless you have good reason to believe the second answer is definitely more correct
11. Cross out original answer if you decide another answer is more accurate; do not erase until you are ready to hand your paper in
12. Answer all questions; guess unless instructed otherwise
13. Leave time for review

   b. Essay questions
     1. Read each question carefully
     2. Determine exactly what is wanted. Underline key words or phrases.
     3. Decide on outline or paragraph answer
     4. Include many different points and elements unless asked to develop any one or two points or elements
     5. Show impartiality by giving pros and cons unless directed to select one side only
     6. Make and write down any assumptions you find necessary to answer the questions
     7. Watch your English, grammar, punctuation and choice of words
     8. Time your answers; don't crowd material

8) Answering the essay question

Most essay questions can be answered by framing the specific response around several key words or ideas. Here are a few such key words or ideas:

M's: manpower, materials, methods, money, management
P's: purpose, program, policy, plan, procedure, practice, problems, pitfalls, personnel, public relations
   a. Six basic steps in handling problems:
     1. Preliminary plan and background development
     2. Collect information, data and facts
     3. Analyze and interpret information, data and facts
     4. Analyze and develop solutions as well as make recommendations
     5. Prepare report and sell recommendations
     6. Install recommendations and follow up effectiveness

   b. Pitfalls to avoid
     1. *Taking things for granted* – A statement of the situation does not necessarily imply that each of the elements is necessarily true; for example, a complaint may be invalid and biased so that all that can be taken for granted is that a complaint has been registered

2. *Considering only one side of a situation* – Wherever possible, indicate several alternatives and then point out the reasons you selected the best one
3. *Failing to indicate follow up* – Whenever your answer indicates action on your part, make certain that you will take proper follow-up action to see how successful your recommendations, procedures or actions turn out to be
4. *Taking too long in answering any single question* – Remember to time your answers properly

IX. AFTER THE TEST

Scoring procedures differ in detail among civil service jurisdictions although the general principles are the same. Whether the papers are hand-scored or graded by machine we have described, they are nearly always graded by number. That is, the person who marks the paper knows only the number – never the name – of the applicant. Not until all the papers have been graded will they be matched with names. If other tests, such as training and experience or oral interview ratings have been given, scores will be combined. Different parts of the examination usually have different weights. For example, the written test might count 60 percent of the final grade, and a rating of training and experience 40 percent. In many jurisdictions, veterans will have a certain number of points added to their grades.

After the final grade has been determined, the names are placed in grade order and an eligible list is established. There are various methods for resolving ties between those who get the same final grade – probably the most common is to place first the name of the person whose application was received first. Job offers are made from the eligible list in the order the names appear on it. You will be notified of your grade and your rank as soon as all these computations have been made. This will be done as rapidly as possible.

People who are found to meet the requirements in the announcement are called "eligibles." Their names are put on a list of eligible candidates. An eligible's chances of getting a job depend on how high he stands on this list and how fast agencies are filling jobs from the list.

When a job is to be filled from a list of eligibles, the agency asks for the names of people on the list of eligibles for that job. When the civil service commission receives this request, it sends to the agency the names of the three people highest on this list. Or, if the job to be filled has specialized requirements, the office sends the agency the names of the top three persons who meet these requirements from the general list.

The appointing officer makes a choice from among the three people whose names were sent to him. If the selected person accepts the appointment, the names of the others are put back on the list to be considered for future openings.

That is the rule in hiring from all kinds of eligible lists, whether they are for typist, carpenter, chemist, or something else. For every vacancy, the appointing officer has his choice of any one of the top three eligibles on the list. This explains why the person whose name is on top of the list sometimes does not get an appointment when some of the persons lower on the list do. If the appointing officer chooses the second or third eligible, the No. 1 eligible does not get a job at once, but stays on the list until he is appointed or the list is terminated.

X. HOW TO PASS THE INTERVIEW TEST

The examination for which you applied requires an oral interview test. You have already taken the written test and you are now being called for the interview test – the final part of the formal examination.

You may think that it is not possible to prepare for an interview test and that there are no procedures to follow during an interview. Our purpose is to point out some things you can do in advance that will help you and some good rules to follow and pitfalls to avoid while you are being interviewed.

What is an interview supposed to test?

The written examination is designed to test the technical knowledge and competence of the candidate; the oral is designed to evaluate intangible qualities, not readily measured otherwise, and to establish a list showing the relative fitness of each candidate – as measured against his competitors – for the position sought. Scoring is not on the basis of "right" and "wrong," but on a sliding scale of values ranging from "not passable" to "outstanding." As a matter of fact, it is possible to achieve a relatively low score without a single "incorrect" answer because of evident weakness in the qualities being measured.

Occasionally, an examination may consist entirely of an oral test – either an individual or a group oral. In such cases, information is sought concerning the technical knowledges and abilities of the candidate, since there has been no written examination for this purpose. More commonly, however, an oral test is used to supplement a written examination.

Who conducts interviews?

The composition of oral boards varies among different jurisdictions. In nearly all, a representative of the personnel department serves as chairman. One of the members of the board may be a representative of the department in which the candidate would work. In some cases, "outside experts" are used, and, frequently, a businessman or some other representative of the general public is asked to serve. Labor and management or other special groups may be represented. The aim is to secure the services of experts in the appropriate field.

However the board is composed, it is a good idea (and not at all improper or unethical) to ascertain in advance of the interview who the members are and what groups they represent. When you are introduced to them, you will have some idea of their backgrounds and interests, and at least you will not stutter and stammer over their names.

What should be done before the interview?

While knowledge about the board members is useful and takes some of the surprise element out of the interview, there is other preparation which is more substantive. It *is* possible to prepare for an oral interview – in several ways:

1) Keep a copy of your application and review it carefully before the interview

This may be the only document before the oral board, and the starting point of the interview. Know what education and experience you have listed there, and the sequence and dates of all of it. Sometimes the board will ask you to review the highlights of your experience for them; you should not have to hem and haw doing it.

2) Study the class specification and the examination announcement

Usually, the oral board has one or both of these to guide them. The qualities, characteristics or knowledges required by the position sought are stated in these documents. They offer valuable clues as to the nature of the oral interview. For example, if the job involves supervisory responsibilities, the announcement will usually indicate that knowledge of modern supervisory methods and the qualifications of the candidate as a supervisor will be tested. If so, you can expect such questions, frequently in the form of a hypothetical situation which you are expected to solve. NEVER go into an oral without knowledge of the duties and responsibilities of the job you seek.

3) Think through each qualification required

Try to visualize the kind of questions you would ask if you were a board member. How well could you answer them? Try especially to appraise your own knowledge and background in each area, *measured against the job sought*, and identify any areas in which you are weak. Be critical and realistic – do not flatter yourself.

4) Do some general reading in areas in which you feel you may be weak

For example, if the job involves supervision and your past experience has NOT, some general reading in supervisory methods and practices, particularly in the field of human relations, might be useful. Do NOT study agency procedures or detailed manuals. The oral board will be testing your understanding and capacity, not your memory.

5) Get a good night's sleep and watch your general health and mental attitude

You will want a clear head at the interview. Take care of a cold or any other minor ailment, and of course, no hangovers.

What should be done on the day of the interview?

Now comes the day of the interview itself. Give yourself plenty of time to get there. Plan to arrive somewhat ahead of the scheduled time, particularly if your appointment is in the fore part of the day. If a previous candidate fails to appear, the board might be ready for you a bit early. By early afternoon an oral board is almost invariably behind schedule if there are many candidates, and you may have to wait. Take along a book or magazine to read, or your application to review, but leave any extraneous material in the waiting room when you go in for your interview. In any event, relax and compose yourself.

The matter of dress is important. The board is forming impressions about you – from your experience, your manners, your attitude, and your appearance. Give your personal appearance careful attention. Dress your best, but not your flashiest. Choose conservative, appropriate clothing, and be sure it is immaculate. This is a business interview, and your appearance should indicate that you regard it as such. Besides, being well groomed and properly dressed will help boost your confidence.

Sooner or later, someone will call your name and escort you into the interview room. *This is it.* From here on you are on your own. It is too late for any more preparation. But remember, you asked for this opportunity to prove your fitness, and you are here because your request was granted.

What happens when you go in?

The usual sequence of events will be as follows: The clerk (who is often the board stenographer) will introduce you to the chairman of the oral board, who will introduce you to the other members of the board. Acknowledge the introductions before you sit down. Do not be surprised if you find a microphone facing you or a stenotypist sitting by. Oral interviews are usually recorded in the event of an appeal or other review.

Usually the chairman of the board will open the interview by reviewing the highlights of your education and work experience from your application – primarily for the benefit of the other members of the board, as well as to get the material into the record. Do not interrupt or comment unless there is an error or significant misinterpretation; if that is the case, do not hesitate. But do not quibble about insignificant matters. Also, he will usually ask you some question about your education, experience or your present job – partly to get you to start talking and to establish the interviewing "rapport." He may start the actual questioning, or turn it over to one of the other members. Frequently, each member undertakes the questioning on a particular area, one in which he is perhaps most competent, so you can expect each member to participate in the examination. Because time is limited, you may also expect some rather abrupt switches in the direction the questioning takes, so do not be upset by it. Normally, a board member will not pursue a single line of questioning unless he discovers a particular strength or weakness.

After each member has participated, the chairman will usually ask whether any member has any further questions, then will ask you if you have anything you wish to add. Unless you are expecting this question, it may floor you. Worse, it may start you off on an extended, extemporaneous speech. The board is not usually seeking more information. The question is principally to offer you a last opportunity to present further qualifications or to indicate that you have nothing to add. So, if you feel that a significant qualification or characteristic has been overlooked, it is proper to point it out in a sentence or so. Do not compliment the board on the thoroughness of their examination – they have been sketchy, and you know it. If you wish, merely say, "No thank you, I have nothing further to add." This is a point where you can "talk yourself out" of a good impression or fail to present an important bit of information. Remember, *you close the interview yourself.*

The chairman will then say, "That is all, Mr. _____, thank you." Do not be startled; the interview is over, and quicker than you think. Thank him, gather your belongings and take your leave. Save your sigh of relief for the other side of the door.

How to put your best foot forward

Throughout this entire process, you may feel that the board individually and collectively is trying to pierce your defenses, seek out your hidden weaknesses and embarrass and confuse you. Actually, this is not true. They are obliged to make an appraisal of your qualifications for the job you are seeking, and they want to see you in your best light. Remember, they must interview all candidates and a non-cooperative candidate may become a failure in spite of their best efforts to bring out his qualifications. Here are 15 suggestions that will help you:

1) Be natural – Keep your attitude confident, not cocky

If you are not confident that you can do the job, do not expect the board to be. Do not apologize for your weaknesses, try to bring out your strong points. The board is interested in a positive, not negative, presentation. Cockiness will antagonize any board member and make him wonder if you are covering up a weakness by a false show of strength.

2) Get comfortable, but don't lounge or sprawl

Sit erectly but not stiffly. A careless posture may lead the board to conclude that you are careless in other things, or at least that you are not impressed by the importance of the occasion. Either conclusion is natural, even if incorrect. Do not fuss with your clothing, a pencil or an ashtray. Your hands may occasionally be useful to emphasize a point; do not let them become a point of distraction.

3) Do not wisecrack or make small talk

This is a serious situation, and your attitude should show that you consider it as such. Further, the time of the board is limited – they do not want to waste it, and neither should you.

4) Do not exaggerate your experience or abilities

In the first place, from information in the application or other interviews and sources, the board may know more about you than you think. Secondly, you probably will not get away with it. An experienced board is rather adept at spotting such a situation, so do not take the chance.

5) If you know a board member, do not make a point of it, yet do not hide it

Certainly you are not fooling him, and probably not the other members of the board. Do not try to take advantage of your acquaintanceship – it will probably do you little good.

6) Do not dominate the interview

Let the board do that. They will give you the clues – do not assume that you have to do all the talking. Realize that the board has a number of questions to ask you, and do not try to take up all the interview time by showing off your extensive knowledge of the answer to the first one.

7) Be attentive

You only have 20 minutes or so, and you should keep your attention at its sharpest throughout. When a member is addressing a problem or question to you, give him your undivided attention. Address your reply principally to him, but do not exclude the other board members.

8) Do not interrupt

A board member may be stating a problem for you to analyze. He will ask you a question when the time comes. Let him state the problem, and wait for the question.

9) Make sure you understand the question

Do not try to answer until you are sure what the question is. If it is not clear, restate it in your own words or ask the board member to clarify it for you. However, do not haggle about minor elements.

10) Reply promptly but not hastily

A common entry on oral board rating sheets is "candidate responded readily," or "candidate hesitated in replies." Respond as promptly and quickly as you can, but do not jump to a hasty, ill-considered answer.

11) Do not be peremptory in your answers

A brief answer is proper – but do not fire your answer back. That is a losing game from your point of view. The board member can probably ask questions much faster than you can answer them.

12) Do not try to create the answer you think the board member wants

He is interested in what kind of mind you have and how it works – not in playing games. Furthermore, he can usually spot this practice and will actually grade you down on it.

13) Do not switch sides in your reply merely to agree with a board member

Frequently, a member will take a contrary position merely to draw you out and to see if you are willing and able to defend your point of view. Do not start a debate, yet do not surrender a good position. If a position is worth taking, it is worth defending.

14) Do not be afraid to admit an error in judgment if you are shown to be wrong

The board knows that you are forced to reply without any opportunity for careful consideration. Your answer may be demonstrably wrong. If so, admit it and get on with the interview.

15) Do not dwell at length on your present job

The opening question may relate to your present assignment. Answer the question but do not go into an extended discussion. You are being examined for a *new* job, not your present one. As a matter of fact, try to phrase ALL your answers in terms of the job for which you are being examined.

Basis of Rating

Probably you will forget most of these "do's" and "don'ts" when you walk into the oral interview room. Even remembering them all will not ensure you a passing grade. Perhaps you did not have the qualifications in the first place. But remembering them will help you to put your best foot forward, without treading on the toes of the board members.

Rumor and popular opinion to the contrary notwithstanding, an oral board wants you to make the best appearance possible. They know you are under pressure – but they also want to see how you respond to it as a guide to what your reaction would be under the pressures of the job you seek. They will be influenced by the degree of poise you display, the personal traits you show and the manner in which you respond.

ABOUT THIS BOOK

This book contains tests divided into Examination Sections. Go through each test, answering every question in the margin. We have also attached a sample answer sheet at the back of the book that can be removed and used. At the end of each test look at the answer key and check your answers. On the ones you got wrong, look at the right answer choice and learn. Do not fill in the answers first. Do not memorize the questions and answers, but understand the answer and principles involved. On your test, the questions will likely be different from the samples. Questions are changed and new ones added. If you understand these past questions you should have success with any changes that arise. Tests may consist of several types of questions. We have additional books on each subject should more study be advisable or necessary for you. Finally, the more you study, the better prepared you will be. This book is intended to be the last thing you study before you walk into the examination room. Prior study of relevant texts is also recommended. NLC publishes some of these in our Fundamental Series. Knowledge and good sense are important factors in passing your exam. Good luck also helps. So now study this Passbook, absorb the material contained within and take that knowledge into the examination. Then do your best to pass that exam.

EXAMINATION SECTION

EXAMINATION SECTION
TEST 1

DIRECTIONS: Each question or incomplete statement is followed by several suggested answers or completions. Select the one that BEST answers the question or completes the statement. *PRINT THE LETTER OF THE CORRECT ANSWER IN THE SPACE AT THE RIGHT.*

1. Which of the following articles in the surrogate's court procedure act is CORRECTLY matched with its *primary* subject?
    I. Article 1 - general
       Article 2 - appeals
       Article 3 - opening safe deposit box
    II. Article 1 - state tax and liability
        Article 2 - jurisdiction and powers
        Article 3 - proceedings, pleadings, and process
    III. Article 1 - general
         Article 2 - jurisdiction and powers
         Article 3 - proceedings, pleadings, and process

   The CORRECT answer is:

   A. I *only*
   B. II AND III
   C. III *only*
   D. I, II, III

   1._____

2. All of the following are accurate statements regarding the surrogate's court procedure act EXCEPT:

   A. The surrogate's court procedure act may be cited as SCPA
   B. A provision of this act may be cited by its number without being preceded either by the word *section* or the symbol *j*
   C. Reference to an article or section without reference to another law shall be deemed to refer to an article or section of this act
   D. The CPLR and other laws applicable to practice and procedure apply in the surrogate's court without *any* exception to the rule

   2._____

3. Which of the following MOST accurately states the clause preceding definitions of commonly used terms in Article 1, 103?

   A. *When used in this act, unless otherwise required by the context, or unless a contrary intent is expressly declared in the provision to be construed, the words, phrases or clauses hereafter shall be construed as follows....*
   B. *When used in this act, even though the context may demand otherwise, and a contrary intent is expressly declared in the provision to be construed, the words, phrases or clauses shall be construed as follows, irrespective of circumstances.*
   C. *When used in this act, the following words, phrases or clauses shall not be construed as follows, even though the context may require it.*
   D. *The lawyer may exercise his discretion in the use of the words, phrases or clauses hereafter, unless otherwise required by the context, irrespective of any declaration of a contrary intent in the provision to be construed.*

   3._____

1

4. The CPLR and other laws applicable to practice and procedure _____ the surrogate's court _____ other procedure is provided by this act.

   A. do not apply in; because
   B. apply in; except where
   C. may be considered null and void; whenever
   D. may be ignored; especially since

5. All of the following are accurate definitions of terms commonly used in the surrogate's court EXCEPT:
   I. *Administrator* - Any person to whom letters of administration have been issued
   Administrator C.T.A. - Any person to whom letters of administration with the will annexed have been issued
   II. *Beneficiary* - Any person entitled to any part or all of the estate of a decedent under a will or in intestacy
   Bequest or legacy - A transfer of personal property by will
   III. *Devise* - When used as a noun, a transfer of real property by will. When used as a verb, to transfer real property by will.
   Devisee - Any person entitled to take or share in the property of a decedent under the statutes governing descent and distribution

   The CORRECT answer is:

   A. I, II, III   B. II, III   C. III *only*   D. II, III

6. In reference to the surrogate's court procedure act, if a lawyer were to use the term *testamentary trustee,* he would be referring to any person

   A. entitled either absolutely or contingently to share as beneficiary in the estate
   B. to whom preliminary letters testamentary have been issued
   C. to whom letters of trusteeship have been issued
   D. granted or deemed to have the power during minority to manage property vested in an infant

7. According to Article 1, §106, *a person under disability* would be the appropriate phrase for a(n)
   I. infant
   II. incompetent or incapacitated person
   III. financially insolvent person
   IV. unknown, confined as a prisoner who fails to appear under circumstances which the court finds are due to confinement in a penal institution

   The CORRECT answer is:

   A. I, II, IV   B. II, III, IV   C. I, II   D. II

8. Article 1, §105 empowers surrogate's courts in each county to make such rules for the conduct of business in its court as it may deem necessary, _____ the statute and _____ the rules and orders of the administrative board and appellate division applicable there.

   A. not inconsistent with; subject to
   B. inconsistent with; subject to
   C. in flagrant violation of; contradictory to
   D. in compliance with; independent of

9. With the exception of a _____, a person entitled either absolutely or contingently to share as a beneficiary in the estate would be deemed a _____, according to Article 1, §103 of the surrogate's court procedure act.

   A. debtor; legatee
   B. testamentary trustee; temporary administrator
   C. creditor; person interested
   D. presumptive distributee;

10. Under Article 2, §211 of the surrogate's court procedure act, the court may exercise jurisdiction *in personam* obtained, or personal jurisdiction over any person in regard to any matter within the subject matter jurisdiction of the court, *only* if

    A. he/she is a domiciliary of the county who dies or disappears
    B. the person dies without leaving a valid will
    C. the person is a fiduciary whose account is settled and adjudicated by decree of the court
    D. on analogous facts in an action in the supreme court, such a person would be subject to the personal jurisdiction of the supreme court

11. According to Article 2 of the surrogate's court procedure act, the surrogate's court of each county will exercise *exclusive jurisdiction* or jurisdiction exclusive of every other surrogate's court over the estate of any *non-domiciliary* of the state who left
    I. property within that county and no other
    II. personal property which since his death, disappearance or internment has come into that county and no other and remains unadministered
    III. a cause of action against a domiciliary of that county for damages for the wrongful death of the decedent
    IV. personal property in another county which is being administered by an ancillary executor

    The CORRECT answer is:

    A. I, IV
    B. II, IV
    C. III, IV
    D. I, II, III

12. Under Article 2 of the surrogate's court procedure act, when an estate or matter falls within the jurisdiction of the surrogate's courts of _____ counties, by virtue of personal or real property of a _____ decedent being within those counties, *concurrent jurisdiction* must be exercised.

    A. two; non-domiciliary
    B. one; domiciliary
    C. two; devisee
    D. three; non-domiciliary

13. The jurisdictional predicate in Article 2, §210 of the surrogate's court procedure act provides that: *The court shall exercise jurisdiction over persons and property as heretofore or hereafter permitted by law.*
    On how many ADDITIONAL bases is the court allowed to predicate jurisdiction?

    A. One
    B. Two
    C. Three
    D. Four

14. A surrogate's court's jurisdiction would *usually* encompass all of the following EXCEPT

    A. jurisdiction of parties and subject matter
    B. presumptive jurisdiction
    C. exclusive jurisdiction
    D. the service of all processes of the court outside the state, especially those unauthorized by law

15. Which of the following does Article 2 of the surrogate's court procedure act classify as powers *incidental* to the court's jurisdiction?
    The power to

    I. open, vacate, modify or set aside any decree or order of the court directing distribution of the property of an estate which was made without knowledge of a will which affects such distribution
    II. sign any decision, decree or order, including orders in transfer and estate tax proceedings
    III. settle the account of a fiduciary of a common trust fund as provided in the banking law
    IV. transfer for trial to the surrogate's court having jurisdiction, any action pending in the supreme court

    The CORRECT answer is:

    A. I, II, III, IV
    B. III, IV
    C. II, IV
    D. I, II, III

16. Article 2, §209 of the surrogate's court procedure act invests the surrogate court with the jurisdictional power to

    A. dismiss any proceeding which the petitioner has neglected to prosecute diligently
    B. modify any order of the court directing distribution of the property of an estate, despite prior knowledge of a will that affects such distribution
    C. entertain any dispute over an *intervivos* trust
    D. supersede the court that first exercises jurisdiction when an estate is within the jurisdiction of the surrogate courts of two or more counties

17. Under Article 2, §206 of the surrogate's court procedure act, the estate of any domiciliary of the county, at the time of his death, disappearance or internment is subject to the _____ jurisdiction of the surrogate court.

    A. *in personam*
    B. concurrent
    C. exclusive
    D. incidental

18. A debt in favor of a non-domiciliary against a domiciliary would be deemed personal property in all of the following EXCEPT the county

    A. where the domiciliary resides
    B. where the non-domiciliary resides
    C. of the situs of the instrument if the debt were evidenced by a negotiable instrument
    D. where, if other than a natural person, the domiciliary has its principal office

19. Given that the surrogate's court's jurisdiction is affected by the locality of certain assets, it may be CORRECTLY assumed that a(n)

    A. insurance policy upon the life of a non-domiciliary decedent shall have the situs of the principal office in the state of the company or corporation issuing the policy
    B. share of stock of a corporation of this state owned by a non-domiciliary is not deemed personal property in the county where the corporation has its principal office
    C. life insurance policy or share of stock owned by a non-domiciliary may not be deemed personal property in the county where the policy or share of stock is situated
    D. insurance policy upon the life of a non-domiciliary decedent shall not have the situs of the principal office in this state of the company issuing the policy

20. According to Article 2 of the surrogate court's procedure act, the surrogate court in the exercise of its jurisdiction, shall _____ all the powers that the supreme court would have in like actions, and the enumeration of powers in the surrogate's court procedure act _____ be deemed exclusive.

    A. have; shall not
    B. not have; shall
    C. have; shall
    D. not have; shall

21. Article 3 of the surrogate's court procedure act contains all of the following provisions EXCEPT

    A. service of process
    B. statute of limitations
    C. who may serve process
    D. designee for person under disability

22. For the purpose of computing the period of limitation under Article 2 of the CPLR, process must be issued and service made upon any respondent within _____ the date of filing the petition, EXCEPT when process is _____ , according to the statute of limitations.

    A. 30 days after; delayed by the respondent's insolvency
    B. 60 days before; served by publication
    C. 3 months of; served by court order
    D. a year of; delayed by the respondent's disability

23. Under Article 3 of the surrogate's court procedure act, a petition MUST include all of the following EXCEPT

    A. the title of the proceeding, the name and domicile of the person to whose estate or person the proceeding relates
    B. the facts upon which the jurisdiction of the court depends in that particular proceeding
    C. if any interested person be a prisoner, the exact nature of his crime and the names and addresses of his victim(s)
    D. as far as they can be ascertained with due diligence, the names and addresses of all the persons interested upon whom service of process is required

24. Process may be served by all of the following EXCEPT

   A. personal delivery to the respondent
   B. court order
   C. publication where the person is alleged to be in a country with which the United States of America is at war or does not maintain postal communication
   D. delivery of a copy of the process to a consular official of the alien's nation if the interest of a non-domiciliary alien in the estate is less than $500

25. According to Article 3, §306 of the surrogate's court procedure act, a citation must substantially set forth all of the following EXCEPT the

   A. name and domicile of the person to whose estate or person the proceeding relates
   B. names of all persons to be served including those who have waived issuance and service of process
   C. object of the proceeding and the relief sought
   D. date when issued

26. Except when otherwise stated, the citation shall be served at least _____ days before the return date if the person is served _____ the state.

   A. 10; within
   B. 10; outside
   C. 20; within the United States, District of Columbia, the Commonwealth of Puerto Rico but outside
   D. 30; within

27. According to Article 3, §309, when service of process is made by personal delivery, it is normally considered to be complete

   A. immediately upon personal delivery to the respondent
   B. a month after the delivery
   C. only after the respondent has participated in court proceedings
   D. a week after the delivery

28. Under Article 3, §310 of the surrogate's court procedure act, who would be permitted to serve process?
   Any person

   A. under 18 years of age
   B. over 18 years of age
   C. over 21 years of age
   D. who is not disabled in any way

29. Proof of service of subpoena or process would be considered to be inadequate if made by a(n)

   A. infant over the age of 16 years
   B. infant under the age of 16 years or an incompetent
   C. person over the age of 16 years but under 21
   D. person who has previously been convicted for forgery

30. When the person to be served is under disability, his/her designee shall assume (with respect to the proceeding while so designated on behalf of such a person) the same powers and duties as a _____ and is _____ to admit service of process.

    A. guardian ad litem; authorized
    B. person unknown; not authorized
    C. non-domiciliary alien; authorized
    D. person alleged to be deceased; not authorized

31. A petition in a particular proceeding may include all of the following EXCEPT

    A. the age, date of birth, names and addresses of a living guardian
    B. the name and address of an adult relative or friend having an interest in the welfare of an incompetent person
    C. the name and address of the institution having the care and custody of an incapacitated person
    D. the names of at least two other persons besides those mentioned who are interested in the application or proceeding

32. All of the following statements in reference to Article 3 of the surrogate's court procedure act may be considered to be accurate EXCEPT: The process of a surrogate's court

    A. must be made returnable before the court from which it was issued, except where otherwise prescribed by law
    B. must be served upon the father, mother, guardian or any adult person having the care of the infant upon whom service of process is being made
    C. shall be issued to the attorney general of the state where it appears that there is no distributee
    D. will admit pleadings even when they are not directed by the court

33. If served by _____ , the service of process would be considered to be complete when _____ unless the court directs otherwise.

    A. mailing or by registered or certified mail; upon the mailing
    B. personal delivery to an unknown person who must not be designated by the court; delivered
    C. publication; on the 21st day after the first publication
    D. any means that the court directs; a verdict is issued

34. Under Article 3 of the surrogate's court procedure act, when more than 25 creditors are parties interested in the proceedings, process may be served by

    A. publication
    B. delivery of a copy of the process if they are natural domiciliaries
    C. mailing a copy of the process to the 10 creditors who can claim seniority in years over the others
    D. mailing a copy of the process to each of them whether or not they be natural domiciliaries

35. The word *surrogate* means MOST NEARLY

    A. judge   B. wise   C. substitute   D. probate

KEY (CORRECT ANSWERS)

1.	C	11.	D	21.	A	31.	D
2.	D	12.	A	22.	B	32.	D
3.	A	13.	B	23.	C	33.	A
4.	B	14.	D	24.	C	34.	D
5.	C	15.	D	25.	B	35.	C
6.	C	16.	A	26.	A		
7.	A	17.	C	27.	A		
8.	A	18.	B	28.	B		
9.	C	19.	A	29.	B		
10.	D	20.	A	30.	A		

TEST 2

DIRECTIONS: Each question or incomplete statement is followed by several suggested answers or completions. Select the one that BEST answers the question or completes the statement. *PRINT THE LETTER OF THE CORRECT ANSWER IN THE SPACE AT THE RIGHT.*

1. Article 20 of the surrogate's court procedure act is PRIMARILY concerned with the proceeding for 1.____

   A. filing an additional bond, to reduce the penalty of a bond or substitute a new bond
   B. the appointment of a fiduciary solely for the purpose of collecting arrears of pay
   C. an order granting funds for the maintenance of an infant
   D. opening a safe deposit box and determining estate tax liability

2. When used in Article 20 of the surrogate's court procedure act, the term *fiduciary* means 2.____
   _____ , where no fiduciary has been appointed.

   A. any person in actual or constructive possession of any property required to be included in the gross estate of the decedent as determined under Article 10-C or Article 26 of the tax law
   B. a person in debt
   C. a creditor of one of the persons interested in the proceedings
   D. a person in actual or alleged possession of property that must be included in the gross estate of the decedent as determined under Article 20 of the surrogate's court procedure act

3. According to Article 20, §2002, under the provisions of the tax law relating to transfer or estate taxes, the surrogate's court of every county having jurisdiction of the estate of a decedent shall have jurisdiction to 3.____

   A. hear and determine all questions arising in the course of the proceedings
   B. partially determine the amount of tax imposed
   C. perform any act that would come within the surrogate's jurisdiction, even one that is unauthorized by law
   D. hear but not determine any questions that may arise in the proceedings

4. If the court has jurisdiction of a decedent's estate and a person, firm or corporation possesses the decedent's papers or safe deposit box that may contain his will, the court may issue an exparte order directing the person, firm or corporation to do all of the following EXCEPT 4.____

   A. permit a person named in the order to examine the papers or safe deposit box
   B. permit the person named in the order to make an inventory of the papers or contents of the safe deposit box in the presence of a representative of the state tax commission
   C. if the decedent's will, deed to his burial plot or insurance policy be found, to deliver the will to the court clerk personally or by registered mail
   D. if the decedent's deed to his burial plot be found, to deliver the deed to a person who need not be designated on the order

5. In order to determine the value of the estate and the amount of tax to which it is liable without appointing an appraiser, the surrogate's court must fulfill all of the following conditions EXCEPT

    A. a petition filed by a fiduciary
    B. a copy of the petition and proposed order served upon the tax commission or its attorney
    C. the original petition, notice of motion, and a copy of the proposed order filed with the clerk in any county which has designated a transfer and estate tax clerk of the court
    D. the provisions of 304 apply to the petition and tax be determined without the consent of the petitioner and the tax commission

6. If the court were to decide that the petition to determine the tax is insufficient, or more than 18 months have passed since the decedent's death without the institution of any proceeding to determine the tax, the court may

    A. direct the appraiser for his county to proceed pursuant to the provisions of Section 249-V of the tax law
    B. declare the estate to be state property
    C. issue a special order directing an appraiser of the estate to withhold his determination of the tax from the court and the decedent
    D. enter an order determining the tax without considering the appraiser's report

7. Article 20, §2008 provides that if the tax commission or fiduciary were dissatisfied with the determination of tax, they would be allowed to appeal to the court within _____ days from the entry of the order and such appeals would be governed by Section _____ of the tax law.

    A. 30; 250-X   B. 60; 249-X
    C. 20; 221-X   D. 30; 220-X

8. Which of the following provisions regarding fees charged in the surrogate's court is/are CORRECT?
    I. Fees for service, filing, and other matters shall be as provided in this article to the exclusion of other statutory provisions unless expressly stated to the contrary.
    II. Clerks' fees shall not be payable in advance.
    III. A compulsory fee is charged for motions made in a pending proceeding or for exparte applications.
    IV. All fees shall be the property of the county, unless otherwise provided by law.
    The CORRECT answer is:

    A. I, II, III, IV   B. II, III, IV
    C. I, IV   D. II, III, IV

9. Upon filing a petition to commence a proceeding, the fee for probate of a will would be computed INITIALLY upon

    A. the gross estate passing by will as stated in the petition
    B. the property outside the state passing under such will
    C. a hypothetical amount that could result from subsequent tax proceeding
    D. projected taxes that could be imposed on the estate

10. Provided that the value of the estate shown by subsequent tax proceeding _____ the value originally stated and upon which the fee was paid, the additional probate fee shall be the _____ the fee based on the value shown by the tax proceeding and the fee which was initially paid.

    A. exceeds; difference between
    B. exceeds; sum of
    C. is less than; difference between
    D. is less than; sum of

11. A fee of $30 would be charged by the surrogate's court in the counties within the City of New York for filing a petition to commence all of the following proceedings EXCEPT under SCPA Section

    A. 607 - punish respondent for contempt
    B. 711 - suspend, modify, revoke letters or remove a custodian or guardian
    C. 717 - suspend powers; fiduciary in war
    D. 2003 - open safe deposit box

12. According to Article 24 which provides a schedule of fees charged to commence proceedings in a surrogate's court, it is TRUE that it costs

    A. more to furnish a transcript of a decree in counties within the City of New York than in all other counties
    B. the same to file a demand for trial by jury in any proceeding and to file objections to the probate of a will, surrogate's court procedure act 1410, in counties other than the City of New York
    C. more to file a petition to commence proceedings for construction of will than to compel production of will in the counties within the City of New York
    D. $10.00 for searching and certifying to any record for which search is made in counties within the City of New York and in all other counties

13. In counties within the City of New York, the fees for searching and certifying to any record are: $30 for a search made for _____ years and $90 for a search made for _____ years.

    A. under 25; over 25   B. under 20; over 20
    C. under 20; 20   D. 10; 30

14. The surrogate's court procedure act, Article 24, 2402 provides that no fee shall be charged for any of the following EXCEPT

    A. filing objections of a guardian ad litem
    B. filing the annual account of a guardian
    C. any certificate or certified copy of a paper required to be filed with the United States Veteran Administration
    D. recording any instrument, decree or other paper which is required by law to be recorded

15. Court proceedings are exempt from any charge when a fiduciary is appointed for all of the following reasons EXCEPT for collecting

    A. interest on money lent by an individual in a private capacity
    B. the proceeds of a war risk insurance policy

C. bounty, arrears of pay, prize money
D. pension dues or other dues or gratuities due from the federal or state government for services of an infant

16. In reference to the schedule of fees for surrogate's court proceedings, which of the following statements are TRUE? No fee shall be charged
    I. for filing a petition in a proceeding for filing an additional bond, to reduce the penalty of a bond
    II. to or received from the State of New York when taking any proceeding with respect to the estate of a person who was a recipient of benefits from social services
    III. for filing a petition for release against the state
    IV. for filing a petition to commence proceedings against a fiduciary
    The CORRECT answer is:

    A. I, II B. III, IV C. I, II, III D. II, III, IV

17. In filing a petition to commence a proceeding for administration in intestacy, in counties within the City of New York, the fee charged would be _____ if the gross value of the estate were _____ according to initial calculations.

    A. $45; less than $10,000
    B. $60; between $10,000 - $20,000
    C. $200; between $25,000 - $50,000
    D. $450; between $500,000 - $800,000

18. According to the schedule of fees in Article 24 of the surrogate's court procedure act, it may be CORRECTLY assumed that for recording _____ the fee rate is _____ all other counties.

    A. any instrument, decree or other paper which is not required by law to be recorded; $3.00 per page in counties within the City of New York and
    B. or filing an authenticated copy of a foreign will; the same in the City of New York and
    C. or filing an authenticated copy of a foreign will; $8.00 per page, $64.00 minimum in counties within the City of New York, and less in
    D. in taxing bill of costs; $1.00 in the City of New York and $10.00 in

19. Which of the following statements regarding fees charged during the surrogate's court procedure would usually be considered to be CORRECT, according to Article 24 of the surrogate's court procedure act?

    A. The fee charged for the filing of a petition shall most likely not include the recording of any decree made in that proceeding which is required by law to be recorded.
    B. Except where otherwise agreed or when special provision is otherwise made by statute, a court reporter is entitled for a copy fully written out from his stenographic notes of the testimony, to 20 cents for each folio.
    C. The court may specifically order that a court reporter's fees for a copy of his stenographic notes of a testimony not be paid out of the estate to which the proceeding relates.
    D. If the surrogate or any personnel of the court goes to a place other than the court to take testimony or to produce records required by law, that person shall be paid his actual and necessary expenses by the party that requires it.

20. Article 28 of the surrogate's court procedure act includes all of the following EXCEPT 20._____

    A. repeal of the surrogate's court act
    B. pending and subsequent actions and proceedings
    C. effective date
    D. appeals

21. *An act in relation to surrogates and the practice and procedure in surrogate's courts* or Chapter _____ of the laws of _____ are repealed by Chapter _____ of the laws of _____, according to Article 28 of the surrogate's court procedure act. 21._____

    A. 928; 1920; 953; 1966
    B. 953; 1966; 928; 1920
    C. 921; 1926; 926; 1966
    D. 928; 1920; 930; 1966

22. According to Article 28, the repealed surrogate's court procedure act, L.1966, c.953, would apply to all of the following EXCEPT 22._____

    A. pending actions
    B. where the court determines that the application in a particular pending action would not be feasible
    C. where the court determines that the application in a pending action would not work injustice
    D. proceedings that are not pursuant to law in an action or proceeding taken prior to the time the act took effect

23. In reference to the repealed surrogate's court procedure act, L.1966, c.953, it may be ACCURATELY stated that: 23._____

    A. This act shall not succeed the surrogate's court act in most cases
    B. This act may not be considered to substitute the surrogate's court act in the statutes and rules of the state
    C. Reference in any statute to a particular provision of the surrogate's court act shall usually be considered to refer to the provision of the repealed act that replaces the prior provision
    D. Reference in any statute to a particular provision of the surrogate's court act shall be considered to refer to the practice that replaces the prior provision, although the prior provision is superseded by a specific provision of this act, L.1966, c.953

24. If any clause, sentence, paragraph, section or part of the repealed chapter of the surrogate's court act were to be judged invalid by a court of competent jurisdiction, such a decree would 24._____

    A. invalidate the remainder of the chapter
    B. not be confined in its operation to the clause, sentence or paragraph in question
    C. impair certain sections of the remainder
    D. not affect, impair or invalidate the remainder and shall be confined in its operation to the clause, sentence, paragraph, subdivision or part directly involved in the controversy

25. According to 2805 of Article 24, the surrogate's court act after repeal took effect on

    A. September 1, 1967
    B. September 1, 1966
    C. December 1, 1966
    D. January 1, 1968

26. Which of the following articles of the surrogate's court procedure act is CORRECTLY matched to a major topic that is discussed in the article?

    A. Article 20 - effective date
    B. Article 24 - appeals
    C. Article 28 - expenses
    D. Article 20 - notice of determination

27. In reference to the notice of determination, it may be ACCURATELY stated that the court shall

    A. immediately forward to the fiduciary who has appeared by attorney any notice of assessment of tax upon any estate
    B. immediately forward to the fiduciary, and if he has appeared by attorney, to his attorney any notice of assessment of tax upon any estate
    C. forward to the tax commission copies of all orders entered by it in relation to the tax on any estate, except for any orders of exemption
    D. not forward to the fiduciary any notice of assessment of tax upon any estate

28. In order to determine the value of the estate and the amount of tax to which it is liable without appointing an appraiser, upon the petition of a fiduciary, a court must fulfill all of the following conditions EXCEPT

    A. a copy of the petition, notice of motion for such determination, and proposed order be served upon the tax commission or its attorney
    B. in any county which has designated a transfer and estate tax clerk of the court, the original petition, notice of motion and proposed order, and a copy of the proposed order be filed with the clerk
    C. the provisions of 304 must apply to the petition
    D. the petition, notice of motion and order shall be upon such forms as may be presented by the tax commission

29. The court may direct the appraiser for the decedent's county to report to the court his determination of estate tax if it appears to the court that

    A. the petition to determine the tax is sufficient to permit a determination to be made
    B. more than 28 months have passed since the decedent's death and no proceeding to determine the tax has been instituted
    C. more than 18 months have passed since the decedent's death and an extension of time to institute a proceeding has been obtained
    D. more than 18 months have passed since the decedent's death and no proceeding to determine the tax has been instituted, and no extension of time to institute a proceeding has been obtained

30. Based on Article 24 of the surrogate's court procedure act, which provides the amount of fees for varied proceedings, it would be CORRECT to assume that in a proceeding for

    A. accounting, where more than one account is filed under a single petition, the fee shall be based separately on the gross value of each separate fund or trust accounted for
    B. a transfer or estate tax upon the estate of a domiciliary, if the decedent was a non-domiciliary, the fee shall not be as shown by the fee schedule in this act
    C. filing an instrument which releases and discharges a fiduciary but does not contain any statement of account, a fee of five dollars shall be charged
    D. recording an instrument which releases and discharges a fiduciary, no fee shall be charged

30.____

31. According to Article 24, 2402 of the surrogate's court procedure act, the fee paid in a probate or ancillary probate proceeding shall include all charges EXCEPT if

    A. probate is uncontested
    B. probate be contested
    C. a jury trial is not required
    D. a note of issue is not filed

31.____

32. In proceedings not otherwise provided in the surrogate's court procedure act, the fee shall _____ determined according to the schedule provided in Article 24, §2402 based on the _____ of the subject matter.

    A. not be; value
    B. be; contents
    C. be; style of presentation
    D. be; value

32.____

33. In counties within the City of New York, filing a petition to commence a proceeding to _____ would cost more than a petition to _____, based on the fee schedule in Article 24.

    A. suspend, modify, revoke letters or remove a custodian or guardian; suspend, modify, revoke letters or remove a fiduciary other than a custodian or guardian
    B. compel production of the will; commence construction of the will
    C. appoint a trustee; appoint a guardian
    D. compel fiduciary to account; continue business

33.____

34. Which of the following CORRECTLY states the title of Chapter 928 of the laws of 1920? A(n)

    A. act in relation to surrogates and the practice and procedure in surrogate's courts
    B. act in relation to fiduciaries and the practice and procedure in surrogate's courts
    C. repeal of surrogate's court act
    D. act in relation to surrogates and the procedure in the supreme court

34.____

35. In reference to Article 20 of the surrogate's court procedures act, which of the following sections is CORRECTLY matched to its primary subject? Section

    A. 2001 - opening safe deposit box
    B. 2008 - appeals
    C. 2002 - definition
    D. 2004 - when additional tax imposable

35.____

KEY (CORRECT ANSWERS)

1.	D	11.	D	21.	A	31.	B
2.	A	12.	C	22.	B	32.	D
3.	A	13.	A	23.	C	33.	C
4.	D	14.	D	24.	D	34.	A
5.	D	15.	A	25.	A	35.	B
6.	A	16.	A	26.	D		
7.	B	17.	A	27.	B		
8.	C	18.	C	28.	C		
9.	A	19.	D	29.	D		
10.	A	20.	D	30.	A		

EXAMINATION SECTION
TEST 1

DIRECTIONS: Each question or incomplete statement is followed by several suggested answers or completions. Select the one that BEST answers the question or completes the statement. *PRINT THE LETTER OF THE CORRECT ANSWER IN THE SPACE AT THE RIGHT.*

1. If a will is properly revoked but a codicil thereto is not, which of the following is true?
    A. The will is considered revoked, but the codicil remains in effect.
    B. The will remains in effect because revocation of the codicil was neglected.
    C. Both are considered revoked.
    D. The revocation of the will is dependent upon the intent of the testator regarding the codicil.

2. Which is not a method by which the Surrogate's Court may obtain jurisdiction over a person?
    A. Service of process upon a party to the action.
    B. Actual appearance of a competent party at a relevant proceeding.
    C. Legal residence of a party of more than 6 months within the county in which the court is located.
    D. By waiver of process.

3. A man, whose last residence was in Brooklyn, died in Manhattan. The decedent's brother lives in Manhattan and filed an action there in Surrogate's Court for appointment as administrator of his brother's estate.
    Which of the following is true?
    A. The New York County Surrogate's Court must transfer the case to King's County.
    B. The New York County Surrogate's Court does not have jurisdiction over the case.
    C. Both New York and King's Counties have jurisdiction over the case because the decedent lived in one county and died in the other.
    D. Neither New York nor King's County has obtained jurisdiction.

4. If proper venue in Surrogate's County may lie in more than one county, by virtue of the fact that a non-domiciliary decedent left property in more than one county, which of the following is true?
    A. Because decedent was not a New York resident, separate actions must be filed in each county in which decedent's property was located, because in the case of non-domiciliaries, only the court of the county in which the property is located can exercise jurisdiction over that property.
    B. A separate action regarding each property may be, but not must be, maintained in each county in which decedent's property is located.
    C. Venue is proper only in the county in which the most valuable of decedent's property is located.
    D. If actions are filed in multiple counties, each of which contains decedent's property, all actions must be transferred to the first county in which such action was filed.

5. A proceeding to appoint a guardian for a mentally incapacitated person may be brought in which of the following courts?
    A. Supreme Court
    B. County Court
    C. Surrogate's Court
    D. Any of the above

6. What is the difference between an executor of an estate and an administrator of an estate?
    A. There is no difference.
    B. An executor is appointed by a testator and an administrator is appointed by a court.
    C. An administrator is appointed by a testator and an executor is appointed by a court
    D. One applies to a non-domiciliary decedent and the other applies to a New York decedent.

7. A certificate of letters of administration duly issued by a Surrogate's court are sufficient evidence of their existence for all purposes for what period of time?
    A. For 6 months after the date of such issuance.
    B. For 90 days after the date of such issuance.
    C. For one year after the date of such issuance.
    D. None of the above.

8. What is the effect on a will of a clause that is contained below the testator's signature?
    A. It is given the same effect as any other clause of the will.
    B. It depends whether it was written before or after the will was executed.
    C. It is given no effect.
    D. It invalidates the will.

9. E-filing of papers in Surrogate's Court is:
    A. Mandatory for all parties represented by an attorney.
    B. Voluntary at all times by any party.
    C. Determined by the manner in which the case was commenced.
    D. Voluntary at all times by any party, except that it becomes mandatory against a party if that party has already agreed to participate in E-filing, and has not given notice to the court and all other parties that it revokes its desire to participate therein.

10. Under the Mental Hygiene Law, who may act as a guardian for an incapacitated person?
    A. A person over the age of 18 years of age.
    B. A corporation.
    C. The Department of Social Services.
    D. All of the above.

KEY (CORRECT ANSWERS)

1. C
2. C
3. A
4. D
5. D
6. B
7. A
8. C
9. D
10. D

EXAMINATION SECTION
TEST 1

DIRECTIONS: Each question or incomplete statement is followed by several suggested answers or completions. Select the one that BEST answers the question or completes the statement. *PRINT THE LETTER OF THE CORRECT ANSWER IN THE SPACE AT THE RIGHT.*

1. A creator is defined as the person who
   A. makes a disposition of property
   B. makes a disposition of cash only
   C. administers a will or trust
   D. is also deemed a beneficiary

2. A demonstrative disposition is defined as a testamentary disposition of property that
   A. is taken out of a specified or identified property
   B. is taken from the will without regard to the other beneficiaries
   C. takes priority over any remaindermen
   D. is taken from a surplus of specified or identified property

3. Which of the following is NOT required in order to be named as a personal representative of a decedent's estate?
   One must be
   A. over the age of 18
   B. competent
   C. not convicted of a felony
   D. a licensed attorney

4. John dies in April, leaving behind a will and two adult children, Jen and Mary. John bequeaths Jen $5,000 from his savings accounts and leaves Mary the remainder of the money in the same account.
   John's disposition is deemed a
   A. demonstrative
   B. diplomatic
   C. domiciliary
   D. related

5. _____ disposition is NOT a type of gift disposition.
   A. General B. Specific C. Residential D. Demonstrative

6. In New York, as opposed to some other states, adopted children take from the decedent's estate as a _____ would.
   A. non-issue heir
   B. natural child
   C. distant relative
   D. last beneficiary

7. A child born out of wedlock is ALWAYS considered to be the natural child of the _____ estate.
   A. father's
   B. mother's
   C. paternal grandmother's
   D. maternal grandmother's

8. What is the amount of the homestead exception? 8.____
   A. $5,500   B. $15,000   C. $25,000   D. $10,000

9. The homestead benefit is designed to benefit the 9.____
   A. surviving spouse and children of the decedent
   B. surviving spouse of the decedent only
   C. children of the decedent only
   D. remaindermen

10. Which of the following is required in order for a will to be valid in the State 10.____
    of New York?
    A. The testator must be of sound mind and memory
    B. The will must be in writing
    C. The will must be signed in front of two attesting witnesses
    D. All of the above

11. Under the Surrogates Court Procedures Act, can a will be probated if it 11.____
    is lost?
    A. No, not under any circumstances
    B. Yes, if he or she can prove by a preponderance of the evidence that the will was not simply misplaced
    C. Yes, if he or she can prove through clear and convincing evidence that the will was lost and not revoked by physical act
    D. Yes, but determined on a case by case basis

12. Under the Estates, Powers, and Trusts Law, a trustee is obligated to exercise 12.____
    reasonable _____ in making investment decisions on the behalf of the trust.
    A. decision, skill, and caution   B. exercise, decision, and caution
    C. care, skill, and decision   D. care, skill, and caution

13. The _____ is the first party granted a letter of administration in an intestate 13.____
    distribution, assuming the party is eligible to qualify?
    A. decedent's children   B. decedent's grandchildren
    C. surviving spouse   D. decedent's siblings

14. Over what amount will a probate proceeding commence when a person 14.____
    dies with a will?
    A. $5,000   B. $20,000   C. $30,000   D. $50,000

15. Probate is defined as 15.____
    A. the process by which assets of the decedent are collected and distributed to the appropriate parties
    B. the process by which the decedent's heirs are named
    C. a formal process where the decedent's heirs are prioritized
    D. a proceeding that determines how much cash is left in the estate

16. Which of the following documents is NOT required to be submitted to the Surrogates Court fully to probate a will?
    A. Waiver and consent
    B. Notice of probate
    C. Probate petition
    D. Subpoena of the trustee

16.____

17. Which of the following parties may petition the Surrogates Court to probate a decedent's will?
    A. A creditor
    B. Any person entitled to letters of administration with the fully annexed will
    C. Any party to an action involving the decedent
    D. All of the above

17.____

18. The waiver of process and consent to process form does not require which of the following information?
    A. The relationship to the decedent
    B. Notary stamp
    C. The date of the decedent's last will and testament
    D. Photo identification

18.____

19. New York acknowledges which of the following with regard to wills, testaments, and codicils?
    A. Handwritten wills
    B. Wills signed by two witnesses
    C. In limited circumstances, oral wills
    D. All of the above

19.____

20. Children born after the execution of a decedent's last will and testament are
    A. entitled to receive what the other children of the testator receives
    B. barred from recovery
    C. cannot receive anything from the will unless specifically named
    D. cannot receive more than a nominal share in trust or estate assets

20.____

21. A surviving spouse's inheritance is determined first by the will of the decedent. However, if no will exists, the surviving spouse's inheritance is determined by the _____ laws of the state.
    A. family   B. intestacy   C. civil   D. criminal

21.____

22. In New York State, a surviving spouse has a right of
    A. disavowal   B. disclaimer   C. election   D. mediation

22.____

23. If a decedent dies with no issue and no surviving spouse, under the intestacy laws of New York State, the next lawful taker are the decedent's
    A. siblings
    B. grandparents
    C. surviving parents
    D. grandchildren, if any

23.____

24. The appropriate venue for a probate proceeding is based on the
    A. domicile of the decedent at the time of death
    B. birthplace of the decedent
    C. place of residence of the decedent for a majority of the year
    D. birthplace of the decedent's issue

24.____

25. An individual can be disqualified to serve as a personal representative on account of which of the following?
    A. Deceitfulness
    B. Carelessness
    C. Substance abuse
    D. All of the above

25.____

KEY (CORRECT ANSWERS)

1.	A	11.	C
2.	B	12.	D
3.	D	13.	C
4.	A	14.	B
5.	C	15.	A
6.	B	16.	D
7.	B	17.	D
8.	D	18.	D
9.	A	19.	D
10.	D	20.	A

21.	B
22.	C
23.	C
24.	A
25.	D

TEST 2

DIRECTIONS: Each question or incomplete statement is followed by several suggested answers or completions. Select the one that BEST answers the question or completes the statement. *PRINT THE LETTER OF THE CORRECT ANSWER IN THE SPACE AT THE RIGHT.*

1. Where are Surrogates Courts located in the State of New York? 1.____
   A. One in every country, with the exception of New York County which has two
   B. Two in every county, including New York County
   C. Five in New York County, where a majority of deaths occur
   D. One in every county

2. A decree of final settlement of an executor's (or administrator's) account cannot be executed unless which of the following has occurred FIRST? 2.____
   A. The estate tax is fully paid.
   B. The Surrogates Court has been notified of the executor's appointment.
   C. The decedent's will has been stamped or otherwise notarized.
   D. The appointment of the administrator is sealed.

3. Before Gabriel's death, he borrowed $5,500 from his neighbor, John. Gabriel died suddenly, but not before he could execute a contract for the loan from John. John has come to Surrogates Court to request that an assignment of interest in Gabriel's estate be established for the $5,000 Gabriel owed him at his death.
   What must John provide to the court to secure his interest? 3.____
   A. Gabriel's death certificate
   B. Gabriel's last will and testament
   C. The contract signed by both parties, evidencing the amount payable to John
   D. The draft contract between John and Gabriel, which was only signed by Gabriel at the time

4. Robert currently acts as the custodian of Joe's fourteen-year-old daughter, Jasmine. Robert has been Jasmine's custodian since Joe passed away last year. However, he is moving to California at the end of the month.
   What is the MOST appropriate action Robert can take, acting in Jasmine's best interest? 4.____
   A. File a petition for the appointment of a successor custodian
   B. Ask Joe's 20-year-old nephew, Jim, to be Jasmine's custodian
   C. Ask Jasmine to file for legal emancipation
   D. Draft a will for Jasmine, leaving her additional money should he pass away while he is in California

5. For a person dying after January 1, 2009, a small estate proceeding may be filed only if the
   A. value of the estate is under $10,000
   B. person died without a will
   C. person owed no real estate taxes
   D. value of the estate is less than $30,000 and the person owned no real estate

5._____

6. Mary is Bill's surviving spouse. In order for her to be entitled to take a share of Bill's estate, Mary must file _____ in Surrogates Court.
   A. a deed of will
   B. Bill's last will and testament
   C. a right of election
   D. Bill's last bank statement

6._____

7. Matt has approached the clerk's desk and asked for a copy of his mother's death certificate. Which of the following statements is CORRECT?
   The clerk
   A. can provide the death certificate once Matt provides proper identification
   B. cannot provide the death certificate without proof that Matt is Mary's lawful son
   C. does not provide death certificates
   D. does not provide death certificates to issue and heirs

7._____

8. What needs to be filed with the probate petition in order to get the will admitted to probate?
   A. The original will and certified copy of the death certificate
   B. The original will only
   C. A photocopy or certified copy of the death certificate
   D. A certified copy of the obituary of the decedent

8._____

9. The Surrogates Court has jurisdiction for which types of guardianship cases? Guardianship
   A. of an infant or developmentally disabled individual
   B. of infants only
   C. of PINS or other delinquents
   D. over those minors who may legally file for emancipation

9._____

10. Voluntarily administration may NOT be used to administer
    A. jewelry   B. cash   C. collectibles   D. real property

10._____

11. Which of the following types of adoptions does the Surrogates Court NOT handle?
    A. Grandparent adoptions
    B. Adoptions of adults over the age of 18
    C. Step-parent and/or remarriage adoptions
    D. Illegal adoptions

11._____

12. An executor is MOST appropriately defined as the person	12.____
    A. in the will who receives the largest benefit
    B. appointed in a will to handle an estate proceeding
    C. who must file estate taxes
    D. appointed in the will to dispose of real property only

13. A spouse can be disqualified as a "surviving spouse" if which of the	14.____
    following is TRUE?
    A. The marriage was previously void.
    B. The widow was older than the deceased.
    C. The widower was older than the deceased.
    D. The marriage was not previously annulled or void prior to the passing of
       the deceased.

14. Katie has been named as executor of her mother's estate. However, she	14.____
    feels that she cannot serve because she is too distraught, upset, and anxious
    about her mother's death.
    What is the MOST appropriate course of action for Katie to undertake in order
    to properly administer her mother's estate?
    Seek to find a(n)
    A. Alternate Executor   B. Successor Executor
    C. Successive Administrator   D. Replacement Executor

15. An individual in an executor or administrator role serves as a	15.____
    A. relative   B. remainderman
    C. fiduciary   D. responsible party

16. The term "issue" refers to a decedent's	16.____
    A. direct descendants, such as children and grandchildren
    B. nuclear family, such as spouse
    C. legacy, as defined by his will
    D. last wishes, as defined by his will and/or codicils

17. Jamie approaches the clerk's desk to ask about the disposition of her	17.____
    grandfather's will. She informs the clerk that she believes her grandfather
    would have left her his coin collection. The executor of her grandfather's will,
    her grandmother, told her that she would be a rightful legatee.
    What is the MOST appropriate response of the clerk?
    A legatee
    A. is someone who inherits personal property
    B. is someone who inherits real property only
    C. cannot inherit coin collections
    D. is not eligible to inherit personal property unless they are also the
       executor of the estate

18. When can a settlor exercise his right to revoke or modify a revocable trust?
    A. At any time
    B. Only after death
    C. At any time during his or her lifetime
    D. At any time during his or her lifetime by orally expressing his or her intent to change their mind

19. A devisee, Adrienne, wants to gift her inheritance to her nephew. Her nephew, however, is a minor.
    How will the devisee's property MOST likely pass to her nephew?
    Adrienne will likely pass the inheritance of _____ to her nephew.
    A. real property by will
    B. cash by will
    C. personal property by trust
    D. jewelry by trust

20. Jamal leaves his home to his daughter, Simone, in his will. Simone tragically passed away in a motor vehicle accident in April. Jamal dies in July and does not update his will prior to his passing.
    Jamal's home is deemed a _____ gift.
    A. recursive
    B. failed
    C. germane
    D. revoked

21. A settlor is someone
    A. who creates a will
    B. who creates a trust
    C. without a large estate
    D. with a small estate

22. A successor trustee is defined as the person who takes over as trustee if the original trustee
    A. dies
    B. moves out of state
    C. is charged with a felony
    D. can no longer serve

23. One way of dividing property among the descendants of the deceased is per capita. The other way is per _____, a Latin term which translates to "right of representation".
    A. representation
    B. rights
    C. stirpes
    D. stripes

24. A custodian is different than a trustee in what way?
    A custodian
    A. manages property inherited by a minor, whereas a trustee has legal authority over assets in a trust
    B. manages property for another, whereas a trustee has legal authority over assets in a trust
    C. has legal authority over assets in a trust, whereas a trustee manages property inherited by a minor
    D. has no legal power in a court

25. Testamentary refers to having to do with a
    A. will
    B. codicil only
    C. trust
    D. minor under the Uniform Transfers to Minors Act

25.____

KEY (CORRECT ANSWERS)

1. A
2. A
3. C
4. A
5. D

6. C
7. C
8. A
9. A
10. D

11. D
12. B
13. A
14. B
15. C

16. A
17. A
18. C
19. A
20. B

21. B
22. D
23. C
24. A
25. A

TEST 3

DIRECTIONS: Each question or incomplete statement is followed by several suggested answers or completions. Select the one that BEST answers the question or completes the statement. *PRINT THE LETTER OF THE CORRECT ANSWER IN THE SPACE AT THE RIGHT.*

Questions 1-7.

DIRECTIONS: Questions 1 through 7 are to be answered on the basis of the following fact pattern.

Timothy's father, Jason, passed away last year. Jason was predeceased by Timothy and two other children. Timothy was not aware that his father had any more children. Jason left Timothy his house and all personal property to his other two children, Amy and Bill. Jason's estate is much larger (roughly $200,000) than Timothy anticipated.

1. Timothy would like to file a small estate proceeding. Why is Timothy unable to file a small estate proceeding?
   Jason's estate exceeds
   A. $30,000   B. $50,000   C. $100,000   D. $130,000

2. Jason's receipt of real property deemed him a
   A. legatee   B. devisee   C. trustee   D. fiduciary

3. Jason's other two children, Amy and Bill, are deemed
   A. void heirs
   B. ab initio decedents
   C. issue
   D. remaindermen

4. The Surrogates Clerk has assessed a filing fee for Jason's estate.
   The filing fee associated with admitting the estate to probate is determined by the
   A. number of children the decedent had
   B. number of rightful heirs the decedent had
   C. size of the estate
   D. property acreage of the decedent's primary residence

5. Amy and Bill's receipt of personal property deems them
   A. devisees
   B. legatees
   C. fiduciary
   D. property beneficiaries

6. If Amy and Bill were adopted by Jason prior to Jason's death, are they still deemed to be Jason's issue?
   A. No
   B. Yes, because issue includes adopted children
   C. Yes, because Jason adopted them prior to death
   D. Yes, but only if Jason mentioned the adoption in his will

7. After discovering that Jason had two more children, Timothy inquires with the Surrogates Court about whether Amy and Bill were formally adopted. Assuming the adoption records are NOT sealed, how can the Surrogates Court assist Timothy?
    A. Timothy can obtain a record of adoption, but only if he knows the county where the adoption took place.
    B. The Surrogates Court can unseal the records based on Timothy's request.
    C. The Surrogates Court can put Timothy in touch with a family law attorney who can further assist in this matter.
    D. The Surrogates Court cannot assist at all in this scenario.

7.____

8. Assuming that Sam dies without a will, leaving behind one daughter and one son, Sam's property is owned by Sam's children _____ at the time of his death.
    A. 60/30   B. bilaterally   C. equally   D. proportionally

8.____

9. Assume that Sam's daughter, Beth, as a daughter named Cara. Sam's son, Bill, has a son named Dave. If Bill dies, who are the rightful owners of Sam's estate?
    A. Beth and Cara only
    B. Cara and Dave
    C. Beth, Cara, and Dave
    D. Beth only

9.____

10. Daniel believes his sister is incompetent and should not be named as executor of their mother's estate. Daniel informs his sister that she is disqualified from acting as executor.
    When is Daniel's decision regarding his sister effective?
    A. Immediately
    B. Six months after Daniel deems his sister to be incompetent
    C. At least one year after Daniel deems his sister to be incompetent
    D. Daniel's decision is ineffective because a person must be judicially declared incapable of managing his or her affairs to be deemed incompetent

10.____

11. In the New York Estates, Powers, and Trusts Law, the term "infant" or "minor" is defined as a person under the age of
    A. 21   B. 19   C. 18   D. 16

11.____

Questions 12-15.

DIRECTIONS: Questions 12 through 15 are to be answered on the basis of the following fact pattern.

Jackson passed away in October of last year. His daughter, Amy, has several questions regarding the administration of his estate. Amy's three younger siblings are all living, but in different parts of the country. Jackson's estate is very large and quite complex. Jackson's assets are held in trust and, before Jackson's death, he appointed a local bank as the Trustee.

3 (#3)

12. Jackson wants to make a distribution to his children per capita. What percentage will each of his four children receive? 12.____
    A. 10% each of his older children, 40% each to his younger children
    B. 25% each to all children, equally
    C. 30% each to his older children, 20% each to his younger children
    D. 100% to his first born only

13. The governing instrument that must be relied upon in administering Jackson's estate can include which of the following? 13.____
    A. Will B. Trust agreement
    C. Testamentary instrument D. All of the above

14. Jackson's youngest child, Saul, is an infant. The petition for appointment of guardianship form requires which of the following? 14.____
    A. Relationship of the petitioner to the adoptee
    B. Name of the infant's grandparents
    C. An attestation regarding whether Saul is Native American
    D. All of the above

15. After approximately one year of administration, Amy starts to believe that the trust containing Jackson's assets is not being administered properly by the trustees. 15.____
    The clerk informs Amy that she can file which of the following forms to petition the court for action against the trustees?
    A. Petition for Compulsory Accounting and Related Relief
    B. Non-Trust Accounting
    C. Firearms Inventory
    D. Summons

16. Which of the following are grounds for contesting a will? 16.____
    A. The will has been revoked
    B. The decedent was incapacitated or incompetent at the time of the will drafting
    C. The will itself is fraudulent
    D. All of the above

17. If an individual contests a will due to mental incapacity of the testator, which of the following would the testator have to NOT understand in order for the petitioner to prevail? 17.____
    A. What the testator owns or what is in their will
    B. The names of the testator's unborn grandchildren
    C. What county the testator's children live in
    D. The middle name of the testator's own grandparents

18. Richard dies without a will. How is it determined how Richard's assets are divided?
    A. The intestacy laws of New York
    B. Richard's last thoughts and actions
    C. Richard's handwritten notes about researching wills
    D. The testamentary declarations made under duress

    18.____

19. If a will is being contested, which of the following generally cannot occur?
    A. Distribution of the decedent's assets
    B. Court proceedings regarding the contest and petition
    C. Gathering of evidence regarding the contest and petition
    D. Discussion with outside legal counsel regarding the court proceedings which may or may not take place

    19.____

20. One of the first expenses that shall be paid by a fiduciary from an estate, before all other debts and claims, is
    A. credit card payments
    B. loan and other unsecured obligations
    C. reasonable funeral expenses
    D. tuition bills

    20.____

Questions 21-25.

DIRECTIONS: Questions 21 through 25 are to be answered on the basis of the following fact pattern.

David died owing a large amount of money to a variety of creditors. David's home, for example, was secured by three different mortgages. David's daughter, Sarah, wants to sell the house to pay off some of David's other creditors.

21. What is the term MOST appropriate for the mortgage lenders?
    A. Judgment debtor   B. Judgment creditor
    C. Judgmentees   D. Unsecured petitioner

    21.____

22. What must the mortgage lenders do in an attempt to prevent the sale of the home?
    File a(n)
    A. verified petition in Surrogates Court to obtain a decree granting leave to issue execution against David's home
    B. accounting to verify David's other obligations
    C. trust accounting form to substantiate David's other creditors and/or liens
    D. petition to issue a summons against Sarah to block her from selling the home

    22.____

23. After the petition has been filed, the Surrogates Court must do which of the following?
    A. Serve process personally or in any other reasonable manner
    B. Deny the petition or accounting accordingly
    C. Research David's other obligations to make a determination of accuracy
    D. Subpoena Sara from discussing the matter publicly

23.____

24. In response to the petition or accounting, Sarah, or the trustee of David's estate, may be required to
    A. issue a complaint
    B. file a response
    C. show cause why the petition or accounting should not be granted
    D. issue an indictment against the mortgage lender

24.____

25. The trustee of David's estate, John, recognizes that there may be another solution to the issue of pleasing all of David's creditors. John relies on Section 1813 of the SCPA, which states, in part, that the court may for good cause authorize a compromise or _____ of any debt, claim, or demand in connection with the settlement of an estate.
    A. settlement   B. disposition   C. issue   D. compounding

15.____

KEY (CORRECT ANSWERS)

1.	A		11.	C
2.	B		12.	B
3.	C		13.	D
4.	C		14.	D
5.	A		15.	A
6.	B		16.	D
7.	A		17.	A
8.	C		18.	A
9.	C		19.	A
10.	D		20.	C

21.	B
22.	A
23.	A
24.	C
25.	D

TEST 4

DIRECTIONS: Each question or incomplete statement is followed by several suggested answers or completions. Select the one that BEST answers the question or completes the statement. *PRINT THE LETTER OF THE CORRECT ANSWER IN THE SPACE AT THE RIGHT.*

1. Although James lived in New York most of his life, he drafted and executed a will while living in Italy during the last few years of his life.
   Which of the following is acceptable proof of James's will for probate purposes according to the SCPA?
   A. The unsigned will
   B. The authenticated copy of the will and establishment of jurisdiction where the will was executed
   C. An authenticated copy of the will only
   D. James's last rent payment or other establishment of jurisdiction

   1.____

2. A trust is defined as
   A. the holding of property, including cash, for another person
   B. a right in property, either real or personal, which is held in a fiduciary relationship by one party for the benefit of another
   C. a trusting relationship between a bank and individual
   D. a bond-building exercise wherein one person invests in stocks and/or real estate for the benefit of another person

   2.____

3. Probate is defined as the
   A. formal legal process which gives recognition to a will and appoints an executor or personal representative to distribute assets to the intended beneficiaries
   B. process that may appoint an executor or personal representative
   C. process that decides whether a will is valid
   D. process that appoints attorneys or other counsel to the estate for administration

   3.____

4. Carol Smith is the executor of her mother's estate.
   How should she sign her name in her fiduciary capacity?
   Carol Smith,
   A. Actor   B. Executor   C. Deceased   D. Released

   4.____

5. The disposition of real property includes which of the following?
   A. Sale   B. Transfer to a spouse
   C. Lease   D. All of the above

   5.____

6. Real property, such as a home, can be disposed of for which of the following reasons?
   A. Payment of administration expenses
   B. Payment of funeral expenses
   C. Payment of estate tax
   D. All of the above

   6.____

33

7. Limits Bank, Inc. has been named as the Corporate Trustee of Ed's estate. Ed's primary residence has been included in his estate. The Bank has requested the sale of Ed's residence to pay for estate expenses. Ed's children have filed a petition to delay the sale of Ed's home until the tenants of the home (Ed's grandchildren) have graduated from college.
   Does the SCPA allow the court to delay the sale of the home?
   A. Under the SCPA, the court may delay the disposition of the home until a later date.
   B. The SCPA does not allow the court to delay disposition.
   C. The SCPA allows the court to delay disposition, but only if the current tenants are paying rent.
   D. The SCPA allows the court to delay disposition, but only if the current tenants are in arrears.

8. After a long and contested court battle over the assets of his grandfather, Eric and Dave have come to an agreement outside of court.
   What document must be filed to give the court notice the actions are no longer moving forward?
   A. A stipulation or statement of discontinuance
   B. A stipulation of ceased actions
   C. A notice for additional time
   D. A notice of proposed settlement

9. After Samantha files an objection to the probate of her uncle's will, she has thirty days to present a(n) _____ in accordance of 1411 of SCPA.
   A. order   B. summons   C. citation   D. indictment

10. Samantha can seek an _____ which must occur within a prescribed time period.
    A. proposal of trial
    B. examination before trial
    C. deposition of trial
    D. direction of trial

11. The Surrogates Court hears which of the following cases?
    A. Probate of wills
    B. Affairs of decedents
    C. Administration of estates, large and small
    D. All of the above

12. Eric approached the clerk's desk and asks if he needs an attorney to handle the estate proceedings of his late sister.
    The LEAST appropriate response from the clerk is:
    A. Eric is not required to, but it is advisable
    B. Estate matters can be very complex, but it is ultimately Eric's choice
    C. Eric should seek additional information prior to deciding whether or not to hire an attorney
    D. Absolutely no

13. Administration proceedings refer to the procedure
    A. for collecting and distributing assets of a person who died without a will
    B. for distributing assets to non-issue heirs
    C. for collecting the names of potential distributes
    D. which settles all the affairs of the decedent

14. Inter vivos trusts are defined as trusts created
    A. after the decedent's death
    B. with the assistance of counsel
    C. during the settlor's lifetime
    D. for the benefit of minor children

15. If the value of the total assets in a decedent's account exceeds $30,000, generally speaking one must
    A. file a full administration or probate proceeding
    B. seek relief from filing a petition from the court
    C. hire outside counsel to administer the estate
    D. file an administration procedure to fully distribute the trust

16. Daniel's father's will was witnessed by one individual, Sam. Sam attests under oath that there was another individual in the room when the will was executed, but that other person must have forgotten to sign the will.
    What can Daniel propose to the court?
    The will
    A. was procured by undue influence
    B. is fraudulent
    C. is legally insufficient
    D. is forged

17. Assume the same facts as in Question 16, but now assume that Sam is a beneficiary of the will.
    If the will is deemed valid, what is the likely outcome of the provision relating to Sam's disposition?
    A. The portion of the will disposing property to Sam is deemed void.
    B. The portion of the will disposing property is open to contest by Daniel only.
    C. The portion of the will disposing property to Sam is unaffected.
    D. The entire will is unaffected by Sam's signature.

18. The Surrogates Court of Richmond County hears adoption cases Monday through Thursday.
    When can forms that must be filed in Court be filed?
    A. Friday only
    B. Monday only
    C. Thursday only
    D. Every business day the Court is open

19. Ivan's father passed away in his apartment in Staten Island. Ivan's father had little to no assets. Ivan wants to request the Surrogates Court's permit to divide Ivan's property among those who have a legal right to inherit from Ivan. What must Ivan file with the Court?
    A. Affidavit of Voluntary Administration
    B. Affidavit of Prospective Petition
    C. Tiny Estate Administration Form
    D. Summons for Court Intervention

19.____

20. Jamal died in Suffolk County, lived in New York, and took annual vacations in Orange County.
    In what county must the probate petition be filed?
    A. New York County
    B. Suffolk County
    C. Orange County
    D. The county where the executor lives

20.____

21. The executor of a will must file the _____ and a certified copy of the _____ with the probate petition.
    A. original will; decedent's last bank statements
    B. death certificate; original will
    C. original will; death certificate
    D. death certificate; decedent's last bank statements

21.____

22. The variable fee schedule, based on the size of the estate administered, ranges from $45 for an estate less than $10,000 to $1,250 for an estate valued at _____ and over.
    A. $250,000   B. $500,000   C. $750,000   D. $1,000,000

22.____

23. Jay's uncle Gary died without a will. Gary did not have a large estate, but he was also not close enough to any family members, so Jay is unsure as to the value of Gary's estate. Gary did, though, have children. Jay wants to file a small estate affidavit and asks the court clerk who is responsible for doing so. Generally, the individual that files the small estate affidavit must be the _____ the decedent.
    A. direct heir of   B surviving spouse of
    C. oldest child of   D. closest distribute to

23.____

24. Under New York law, foster children and stepchildren cannot inherit under a will unless they
    A. are of age and competent
    B. lived with the decedent at the time of his or her death
    C. were legally adopted before the decedent's death
    D. were minors at the time of the decedent's death

24.____

25. At the time of Brian's death, he did not have any surviving children. Brian never married.
 Who will inherit Brian's assets assuming he died intestate?
 A. Brian's parents
 B. Brian's siblings
 C. Brian's grandchildren
 D. Brian's co-workers

25.____

KEY (CORRECT ANSWERS)

1. B
2. B
3. A
4. B
5. D

6. D
7. A
8. A
9. C
10. B

11. D
12. D
13. A
14. C
15. A

16. C
17. A
18. D
19. A
20. A

21. C
22. B
23. D
24. C
25. A

EXAMINATION SECTION
TEST 1

DIRECTIONS: Each question or incomplete statement is followed by several suggested answers or completions. Select the one that BEST answers the question or completes the statement. *PRINT THE LETTER OF THE CORRECT ANSWER IN THE SPACE AT THE RIGHT.*

Questions 1-9.

DIRECTIONS: Questions 1 through 9 consist of sentences which may or may not be examples of good English usage. Consider grammar, punctuation, spelling, capitalization, awkwardness, etc. Examine each sentence, and then choose the correct statement about it from the four choices below it. If the English usage in the sentence given is better than it would be with any of the changes suggested in options B, C, and D, choose option A. Do not choose an option that will change the meaning of the sentence.

1. According to Judge Frank, the grocer's sons found guilty of assault and sentenced last Thursday.   1.____

    A. This is an example of acceptable writing.
    B. A comma should be placed after the word *sentenced.*
    C. The word *were* should be placed after *sons*
    D. The apostrophe in *grocer's* should be placed after the *s.*

2. The department heads assistant said that the stenographers should type duplicate copies of all contracts, leases, and bills.   2.____

    A. This is an example of acceptable writing.
    B. A comma should be placed before the word *contracts.*
    C. An apostrophe should be placed before the *s* in *heads.*
    D. Quotation marks should be placed before *the stenographers* and after *bills.*

3. The lawyers questioned the men to determine who was the true property owner?   3.____

    A. This is an example of acceptable writing.
    B. The phrase *questioned the men* should be changed to *asked the men questions.*
    C. The word *was* should be changed to *were.*
    D. The question mark should be changed to a period.

4. The terms stated in the present contract are more specific than those stated in the previous contract.   4.____

    A. This is an example of acceptable writing.
    B. The word *are* should be changed to *is.*
    C. The word *than* should be changed to *then.*
    D. The word *specific* should be changed to *specified.*

5. Of the lawyers considered, the one who argued more skillful was chosen for the job.   5.____

    A. This is an example of acceptable writing.
    B. The word *more* should be replaced by the word *most.*
    C. The word *skillful* should be replaced by the word *skillfully,*
    D. The word *chosen* should be replaced by the word *selected.*

6. Each of the states has a court of appeals; some states have circuit courts.

   A. This is an example of acceptable writing.
   B. The semi-colon should be changed to a comma.
   C. The word *has* should be changed to *have*.
   D. The word *some* should be capitalized.

7. The court trial has greatly effected the child's mental condition.

   A. This is an example of acceptable writing.
   B. The word *effected* should be changed to *affected*.
   C. The word *greatly* should be placed after *effected*.
   D. The apostrophe in *child's* should be placed after the *s*.

8. Last week, the petition signed by all the officers was sent to the Better Business Bureau.

   A. This is an example of acceptable writing.
   B. The phrase *last week* should be placed after *officers*.
   C. A comma should be placed after *petition*.
   D. The word *was* should be changed to *were*.

9. Mr. Farrell claims that he requested form A-12, and three booklets describing court procedures.

   A. This is an example of acceptable writing.
   B. The word *that* should be eliminated.
   C. A colon should be placed after *requested*.
   D. The comma after *A-12* should be eliminated.

Questions 10-21.

DIRECTIONS: Questions 10 through 21 contain a word in capital letters followed by four suggested meanings of the word. For each question, choose the BEST meaning for the word in capital letters.

10. SIGNATORY - A

    A. lawyer who draws up a legal document
    B. document that must be signed by a judge
    C. person who signs a document
    D. true copy of a signature

11. RETAINER - A

    A. fee paid to a lawyer for his services
    B. document held by a third party
    C. court decision to send a prisoner back to custody pending trial
    D. legal requirement to keep certain types of files

12. BEQUEATH - To

    A. receive assistance from a charitable organization
    B. give personal property by will to another
    C. transfer real property from one person to another
    D. receive an inheritance upon the death of a relative

13. RATIFY - To   13._____

    A. approve and sanction   B. forego
    C. produce evidence   D. summarize

14. CODICIL - A   14._____

    A. document introduced in evidence in a civil action
    B. subsection of a law
    C. type of legal action that can be brought by a plaintiff
    D. supplement or an addition to a will

15. ALIAS   15._____

    A. Assumed name   B. In favor of
    C. Against   D. A writ

16. PROXY - A(n)   16._____

    A. phony document in a real estate transaction
    B. opinion by a judge of a civil court
    C. document containing appointment of an agent
    D. summons in a lawsuit

17. ALLEGED   17._____

    A. Innocent   B. Asserted
    C. Guilty   D. Called upon

18. EXECUTE - To   18._____

    A. complete a legal document by signing it
    B. set requirements
    C. render services to a duly elected executive of a municipality
    D. initiate legal action such as a lawsuit

19. NOTARY PUBLIC - A   19._____

    A. lawyer who is running for public office
    B. judge who hears minor cases
    C. public officer, one of whose functions is to administer oaths
    D. lawyer who gives free legal services to persons unable to pay

20. WAIVE - To   20._____

    A. disturb a calm state of affairs
    B. knowingly renounce a right or claim
    C. pardon someone for a minor fault
    D. purposely mislead a person during an investigation

21. ARRAIGN - To   21._____

    A. prevent an escape   B. defend a prisoner
    C. verify a document   D. accuse in a court of law

Questions 22-40.

DIRECTIONS: Questions 22 through 40 each consist of four words which may or may not be spelled correctly. If you find an error in
only one word, mark your answer A;
any two words, mark your answer B;
any three words, mark your answer C;
none of these words, mark your answer D.

22.	occurrence	Febuary	privilege	similiar	22._____
23.	separate	transferring	analyze	column	23._____
24.	develop	license	bankrupcy	abreviate	24._____
25.	subpoena	arguement	dissolution	foreclosure	25._____
26.	exaggerate	fundamental	significance	warrant	26._____
27.	citizen	endorsed	marraige	appraissal	27._____
28.	precedant	univercity	observence	preliminary	28._____
29.	stipulate	negligence	judgment	prominent	29._____
30.	judisial	whereas	release	guardian	30._____
31.	appeal	larcenny	transcrip	jurist	31._____
32.	petition	tenancy	agenda	insurance	32._____
33.	superfical	premise	morgaged	maintainance	33._____
34.	testamony	publically	installment	possessed	34._____
35.	escrow	decree	eviction	miscelaneous	35._____
36.	securitys	abeyance	adhere	corporate	36._____
37.	kaleidoscope	anesthesia	vermilion	tafetta	37._____
38.	congruant	barrenness	plebescite	vigilance	38._____
39.	picnicing	promisory	resevoir	omission	39._____
40.	supersede	banister	wholly	seize	40._____

KEY (CORRECT ANSWERS)

1. C	11. A	21. D	31. B
2. C	12. B	22. B	32. D
3. D	13. A	23. D	33. C
4. A	14. D	24. B	34. B
5. C	15. A	25. A	35. A
6. A	16. C	26. D	36. A
7. B	17. B	27. B	37. A
8. A	18. A	28. C	38. B
9. D	19. C	29. D	39. C
10. C	20. B	30. A	40. D

EXAMINATION SECTION
TEST 1

DIRECTIONS: Each question or incomplete statement is followed by several suggested answers or completions. Select the one that BEST answers the question or completes the statement. *PRINT THE LETTER OF THE CORRECT ANSWER IN THE SPACE AT THE RIGHT.*

Questions 1-6.

DIRECTIONS: Questions 1 through 6 consist of descriptions of material to which a filing designation must be assigned.

Assume that the matters and cases described in the questions were referred for handling to a government legal office which has its files set up according to these file designations. The file designation consists of a number of characters and punctuation marks as described below.

The first character refers to agencies whose legal work is handled by this office. These agencies are numbered consecutively in the order in which they first submit a matter for attention, and are identified in an alphabetical card index. To date numbers have been assigned to agencies as follows:

Department of Correction	1
Police Department	2
Department of Traffic	3
Department of Consumer Affairs	4
Commission on Human Rights	5
Board of Elections	6
Department of Personnel	7
Board of Estimate	8

The second character is separated from the first character by a dash. The second character is the last digit of the year in which a particular lawsuit or matter is referred to the legal office.

The third character is separated from the second character by a colon and may consist of either of the following:

I. A sub-number assigned to each lawsuit to which the agency is a party. Lawsuits are numbered consecutively regardless of year. (Lawsuits are brought by or against agency heads rather than agencies themselves, but references are made to agencies for the purpose of simplification.)

or II. A capital letter assigned to each matter other than a lawsuit according to subject, the subject being identified in an alphabetical index. To date, letters have been assigned to subjects as follows:

Citizenship	A	Housing	E
Discrimination	B	Gambling	F
Residence Requirements	C	Freedom of Religion	G
Civil Service Examinations	D		

2 (#1)

These referrals are numbered consecutively regardless of year. The first referral by a particular agency on citizenship, for example, would be designated A1, followed by A2, A3, etc.

If no reference is made in a question as to how many letters involving a certain subject or how many lawsuits have been referred by an agency, assume that it is the first.

For each question, choose the file designation which is MOST appropriate for filing the material described in the question.

1. In January 2010, two candidates in a 2009 civil service examination for positions with the Department of Correction filed a suit against the Department of Personnel seeking to set aside an educational requirement for the title.
   The Department of Personnel immediately referred the lawsuit to the legal office for handling.

   A. 1-9:1   B. 1-0:D1   C. 7-9:D1   D. 7-0:1

   1._____

2. In 2014, the Police Department made its sixth request for an opinion on whether an employee assignment proposed for 2015 could be considered discriminatory.

   A. 2-5:1-B6   B. 2-4:6   C. 2-4:1-B6   D. 2-4:B6

   2._____

3. In 2015, a lawsuit was brought by the Bay Island Action Committee against the Board of Estimate in which the plaintiff sought withdrawal of approval of housing for the elderly in the Bay Island area given by the Board in 2015.

   A. 8-3:1   B. 8-5:1   C. 8-3:B1   D. 8-5:E1

   3._____

4. In December 2014, community leaders asked the Police Department to ban outdoor meetings of a religious group on the grounds that the meetings were disrupting the area. Such meetings had been held from time to time during 2014. On January 31, 2015, the Police Department asked the government legal office for an opinion on whether granting this request would violate the worshippers' right to freedom of religion.

   A. 2-4:G-1   B. 2-5:G1   C. 2-5:B-1   D. 2-4:B1

   4._____

5. In 2014, a woman filed suit against the Board of Elections. She alleged that she had not been permitted to vote at her usual polling place in the 2013 election and had been told she was not registered there. She claimed that she had always voted there and that her record card had been lost. This was the fourth case of its type for this agency.

   A. 6-4:4   B. 6-3:C4   C. 3-4:6   D. 6-3:4

   5._____

6. A lawsuit was brought in 2011 by the Ace Pinball Machine Company against the Commissioner of Consumer Affairs. The lawsuit contested an ordinance which banned the use of pinball machines on the ground that they are gambling devices.
   This was the third lawsuit to which the Department of Consumer Affairs was a party.

   A. 4-1:1   B. 4-3:F1   C. 4-1:3   D. 3F-4:1

   6._____

7. You are instructed by your supervisor to type a statement that must be signed by the person making the statement and by three witnesses to the signature. The typed statement will take two pages and will leave no room for signatures if the normal margin is maintained at the bottom of the second page.
   In this situation, the PREFERRED method is to type

   A. the signature lines below the normal margin on the second page
   B. nothing further and have the witnesses sign without a typed signature line
   C. the signature lines on a third page
   D. some of the text and the signature lines on a third page

8. Certain legal documents always begin with a statement of venue - that is, the county and state in which the document is executed. This is usually boxed with a parentheses or colons.
   The one of the following documents that ALWAYS bears a statement of venue in a prominent position at its head is a(n)

   A. affidavit
   B. memorandum of law
   C. contract of sale
   D. will

9. A court stenographer is to take stenographic notes and transcribe the statements of a person under oath. The person has a heavy accent and speaks in ungrammatical and broken English.
   When he or she is transcribing the testimony, of the following, the BEST thing for them to do is to

   A. transcribe the testimony exactly as spoken, making no grammatical changes
   B. make only the grammatical changes which would clarify the client's statements
   C. make all grammatical changes so that the testimony is in standard English form
   D. ask the client's permission before making any grammatical changes

10. When the material typed on a printed form does not fill the space provided, a Z-ruling is frequently drawn to fill up the unused space.
    The MAIN purpose of this practice is to

    A. make the document more pleasing to the eye
    B. indicate that the preceding material is correct
    C. insure that the document is not altered
    D. show that the lawyer has read it

11. After you had typed an original and five copies of a certain document, some changes were made in ink on the original and were initialed by all the parties. The original was signed by all the parties, and the signatures were notarized.
    Which of the following should *generally* be typed on the copies BEFORE filing the original and the copies? The inked changes

    A. but not the signatures, initials, or notarial data
    B. the signatures and the initials but not the notarial data
    C. and the notarial data but not the signatures or initials
    D. the signatures, the initials, and the notarial data

12. The first paragraph of a noncourt agreement *generally* contains all of the following EXCEPT the

    A. specific terms of the agreement
    B. date of the agreement
    C. purpose of the agreement
    D. names of the parties involved

13. When typing an answer in a court proceeding, the place where the word ANSWER should be typed on the first page of the document is

    A. at the upper left-hand corner
    B. below the index number and to the right of the box containing the names of the parties to the action
    C. above the index number and to the right of the box containing the names of the parties to the action
    D. to the left of the names of the attorneys for the defendant

14. Which one of the following statements BEST describes the legal document called an acknowledgment?
    It is

    A. an answer to an affidavit
    B. a receipt issued by the court when a document is filed
    C. proof of service of a summons
    D. a declaration that a signature is valid

15. Suppose you typed the original and three copies of a legal document which was dictated by an attorney in your office. He has already signed the original copy, and corrections have been made on all copies.
    Regarding the copies, which one of the following procedures is the PROPER one to follow?

    A. Leave the signature line blank on the copies
    B. Ask the attorney to sign the copies
    C. Print or type the attorney's name on the signature line on the copies
    D. Sign your name to the copies followed by the attorney's initials

16. Suppose your office is defending a particular person in a court action. This person comes to the office and asks to see some of the lawyer's working papers in his file. The lawyer assigned to the case is out of the office at the time.
    You SHOULD

    A. permit him to examine his entire file as long as he does not remove any materials from it
    B. make an appointment for the caller to come back later when the lawyer will be there
    C. ask him what working papers he wants to see and show him only those papers
    D. tell him that he needs written permission from the lawyer in order to see any records

17. Suppose that you receive a phone call from an official who is annoyed about a letter from your office which she just received. The lawyer who dictated the letter is not in the office at the moment.
    Of the following, the BEST action for you to take is to

    A. explain that the lawyer is out but that you will ask the lawyer to return her call when he returns
    B. take down all of the details of her complaint and tell her that you will get back to her with an explanation
    C. refer to the proper file so that you can give her an explanation of the reasons for the letter over the phone
    D. make an appointment for her to stop by the office to speak with the lawyer

17.____

18. Suppose that you have taken dictation for an interoffice memorandum. You are asked to prepare it for distribution to four lawyers in your department whose names are given to you. You will type an original and make four copies. Which one of the following is CORRECT with regard to the typing of the lawyers' names?
    The names of all of the lawyers should appear

    A. *only* on the original
    B. on the original and each copy should have the name of one lawyer
    C. on each of the copies but not on the original
    D. on the original and on all of the copies

18.____

19. Regarding the correct typing of punctuation, the GENERALLY accepted practice is that there should be

    A. two spaces after a semi-colon
    B. one space before an apostrophe used in the body of a word
    C. no space between parentheses and the matter enclosed
    D. one space before and after a hyphen

19.____

20. Suppose you have just completed typing an original and two copies of a letter requesting information. The original is to be signed by a lawyer in your office. The first copy is for the files, and the second is to be used as a reminder to follow up.
    The PROPER time to file the file copy of the letter is

    A. after the letter has been signed and corrections have been made on the copies
    B. before you take the letter to the lawyer for his signature
    C. after a follow-up letter has been sent
    D. after a response to the letter has been received

20.____

21. A secretary in a legal office has just typed a letter. She has typed the copy distribution notation on the copies to indicate *blind copy distribution*. This *blind copy* notation shows that

    A. copies of the letter are being sent to persons that the addressee does not know
    B. copies of the letter are being sent to other persons without the addressee's knowledge
    C. a copy of the letter will be enlarged for a legally blind person
    D. a copy of the letter is being given as an extra copy to the addressee

21.____

22. Suppose that one of the attorneys in your office dictates material to you without indicating punctuation. He has asked that you give him, as soon as possible, a single copy of a rough draft to be triple-spaced so that he can make corrections.
Of the following, what is the BEST thing for you to do in this situation?

    A. Assume that no punctuation is desired in the material
    B. Insert the punctuation as you type the rough draft
    C. Transcribe the material exactly as dictated, but attach a note to the attorney stating your suggested changes
    D. Before you start to type the draft, tell the attorney you want to read back your notes so that he can indicate punctuation

23. When it is necessary to type a mailing notation such as CERTIFIED, REGISTERED, or FEDEX on an envelope, the GENERALLY accepted place to type it is

    A. directly above the address
    B. in the area below where the stamp will be affixed
    C. in the lower left-hand corner
    D. in the upper left-hand corner

24. When taking a citation of a case in shorthand, which of the following should you write FIRST if you are having difficulty keeping up with the dictation?

    A. Volume and page number
    B. Title of volume
    C. Name of plaintiff
    D. Name of defendant

25. All of the following abbreviations and their meanings are correctly paired EXCEPT

    A. viz. - namely
    B. ibid. - refer
    C. n.b. - note well
    D. q.v. - which see

KEY (CORRECT ANSWERS)

1.	D	11.	D
2.	D	12.	A
3.	B	13.	B
4.	B	14.	D
5.	A	15.	C
6.	C	16.	B
7.	D	17.	A
8.	A	18.	D
9.	A	19.	C
10.	C	20.	A

21. B
22. B
23. B
24. A
25. B

EXAMINATION SECTION
TEST 1

DIRECTIONS: Each question or incomplete statement is followed by several suggested answers or completions. Select the one that BEST answers the question or completes the statement. *PRINT THE LETTER OF THE CORRECT ANSWER IN THE SPACE AT THE RIGHT.*

Questions 1-50.

DIRECTIONS: Each of Questions 1 through 50 consists of a word in capital letters followed by four suggested meanings of the word. For each question, choose the word or phrase which means MOST NEARLY the same as the word in capital letters.

1. ABUT
   A. abandon   B. assist   C. border on   D. renounce

2. ABSCOND
   A. draw in   B. give up
   C. refrain from   D. deal off

3. BEQUEATH
   A. deaden   B. hand down   C. make sad   D. scold

4. BOGUS
   A. sad   B. false   C. shocking   D. stolen

5. CALAMITY
   A. disaster   B. female   C. insanity   D. patriot

6. COMPULSORY
   A. binding   B. ordinary   C. protected   D. ruling

7. CONSIGN
   A. agree with   B. benefit
   C. commit   D. drive down

8. DEBILITY
   A. failure   B. legality
   C. quality   D. weakness

9. DEFRAUD
   A. cheat   B. deny
   C. reveal   D. tie

10. DEPOSITION
    A. absence   B. publication
    C. removal   D. testimony

11. DOMICILE
    A. anger   B. dwelling
    C. tame   D. willing

12. HEARSAY
    A. selfish   B. serious   C. rumor   D. unlikely

13. HOMOGENEOUS
    A. human   B. racial   C. similar   D. unwise

14. ILLICIT
    A. understood   B. uneven   C. unkind   D. unlawful

15. LEDGER
    A. book of accounts   B. editor
    C. periodical   D. shelf

16. NARRATIVE
    A. gossip   B. natural   C. negative   D. story

17. PLAUSIBLE
    A. reasonable   B. respectful   C. responsible   D. rightful

18. RECIPIENT
    A. absentee   B. receiver   C. speaker   D. substitute

19. SUBSTANTIATE
    A. appear for   B. arrange
    C. confirm   D. combine

20. SURMISE
    A. aim   B. break   C. guess   D. order

21. ALTER EGO
    A. business partner   B. confidential friend
    C. guide   D. subconscious conflict

22. FOURTH ESTATE
    A. the aristocracy   B. the clergy
    C. the judiciary   D. the newspapers

23. IMPEACH
    A. accuse   B. find guilty
    C. remove   D. try

24. PROPENSITY
    A. dislike   B. helpfulness
    C. inclination   D. supervision

25. SPLENETIC
    A. charming   B. peevish   C. shining   D. sluggish

26. SUBORN
    A. bribe someone to commit perjury
    B. demote someone several levels in rank
    C. deride
    D. substitute

27. TALISMAN
    A. charm
    B. juror
    C. prayer shawl
    D. native

28. VITREOUS
    A. corroding
    B. glassy
    C. nourishing
    D. sticky

29. WRY
    A. comic
    B. grained
    C. resilient
    D. twisted

30. SIGNATORY
    A. lawyer who draws up a legal document
    B. document that must be signed by a judge
    C. person who signs a document
    D. true copy of a signature

31. RETAINER
    A. fee paid to a lawyer for his services
    B. document held by a third party
    C. court decision to send a prisoner back to custody pending trial
    D. legal requirement to keep certain types of files

32. BEQUEATH
    A. to receive assistance from a charitable organization
    B. to give personal property by will to another
    C. to transfer real property from one person to another
    D. to receive an inheritance upon the death of a relative

33. RATIFY
    A. approve and sanction
    B. forego
    C. produce evidence
    D. summarize

34. CODICIL
    A. document introduced in evidence in a civil action
    B. subsection of a law
    C. type of legal action that can be brought by a plaintiff
    D. supplement or an addition to a will

35. ALIAS
    A. assumed name
    B. in favor of
    C. against
    D. a writ

36. PROXY
    A. a phony document in a real estate transaction
    B. an opinion by a judge of a civil court
    C. a document containing appointment of an agent
    D. a summons in a lawsuit

37. ALLEGED
    A. innocent
    B. asserted
    C. guilty
    D. called upon

38. EXECUTE
    A. to complete a legal document by signing it
    B. to set requirements
    C. to render services to a duly elected executive of a municipality
    D. to initiate legal action such as a lawsuit

39. NOTARY PUBLIC
    A. lawyer who is running for public office
    B. judge who hears minor cases
    C. public officer, one of whose functions is to administer oaths
    D. lawyer who gives free legal services to persons unable to pay

40. WAIVE
    A. to disturb a calm state of affairs
    B. to knowingly renounce a right or claim
    C. to pardon someone for a minor fault
    D. to purposely mislead a person during an investigation

41. ARRAIGN
    A. to prevent an escape
    B. to defend a prisoner
    C. to verify a document
    D. to accuse in a court of law

42. VOLUNTARY
    A. by free choice
    B. necessary
    C. important
    D. by design

43. INJUNCTION
    A. act of prohibiting
    B. process of inserting
    C. means of arbitrating
    D. freedom of action

44. AMICABLE
    A. compelled
    B. friendly
    C. unimportant
    D. insignificant

45. CLOSED SHOP
    A. one that employs only members of a union
    B. one that employs union members and unaffiliated employees
    C. one that employs only employees with previous experience
    D. one that employs skilled and unskilled workers

46. ABDUCT
    A. lead
    B. kidnap
    C. sudden
    D. worthless

47. BIAS
    A. ability
    B. envy
    C. prejudice
    D. privilege

48. COERCE
    A. cancel
    B. force
    C. rescind
    D. rugged

49. CONDONE   49.____
    A. combine   B. pardon   C. revive   D. spice
50. CONSISTENCY   50.____
    A. bravery   B. readiness
    C. strain   D. uniformity

KEY (CORRECT ANSWERS)

1. C	11. B	21. B	31. A	41. D
2. D	12. C	22. D	32. B	42. A
3. B	13. C	23. A	33. A	43. A
4. B	14. D	24. C	34. D	44. B
5. A	15. A	25. B	35. A	45. A
6. A	16. D	26. A	36. C	46. B
7. C	17. A	27. A	37. B	47. C
8. D	18. B	28. B	38. A	48. B
9. A	19. C	29. D	39. C	49. B
10. D	20. C	30. C	40. B	50. D

TEST 2

DIRECTIONS: Each question or incomplete statement is followed by several suggested answers or completions. Select the one that BEST answers the question or completes the statement. *PRINT THE LETTER OF THE CORRECT ANSWER IN THE SPACE AT THE RIGHT.*

1. In the sentence, *The prisoner was fractious when brought to the station house*, the word *fractious* means MOST NEARLY
   - A. penitent
   - B. talkative
   - C. irascible
   - D. broken-hearted

2. In the sentence, *The judge was implacable when the attorney pleaded for leniency*, the word *implacable* means MOST NEARLY
   - A. inexorable
   - B. disinterested
   - C. inattentive
   - D. indifferent

3. In the sentence, *The court ordered the mendacious statements stricken from the record*, the word *mendacious* means MOST NEARLY
   - A. begging
   - B. lying
   - C. threatening
   - D. lengthy

4. In the sentence, *The district attorney spoke in a strident voice*, the word *strident* means MOST NEARLY
   - A. loud
   - B. harsh-sounding
   - C. sing-song
   - D. low

5. In the sentence, *The speaker had a predilection for long sentences*, the word *predilection* means MOST NEARLY
   - A. aversion
   - B. talent
   - C. propensity
   - D. diffidence

6. A person who has an uncontrollable desire to steal without need is called a
   - A. dipsomaniac
   - B. kleptomaniac
   - C. monomaniac
   - D. pyromaniac

7. In the sentence, *Malice was immanent in all his remarks*, the word *immanent* means MOST NEARLY
   - A. elevated
   - B. inherent
   - C. threatening
   - D. foreign

8. In the sentence, *The extant copies of the document were found in the safe*, the word *extant* means MOST NEARLY
   - A. existing
   - B. original
   - C. forged
   - D. duplicate

9. In the sentence, *The recruit was more complaisant after the captain spoke to him*, the word *complaisant* means MOST NEARLY
   - A. calm
   - B. affable
   - C. irritable
   - D. confident

10. In the sentence, *The man was captured under highly creditable circumstances*, the word *creditable* means MOST NEARLY
    A. doubtful
    B. believable
    C. praiseworthy
    D. unexpected

11. In the sentence, *His superior officers were more sagacious than he*, the word *sagacious* means MOST NEARLY
    A. shrewd
    B. obtuse
    C. absurd
    D. verbose

12. In the sentence, *He spoke with impunity*, the word *impunity* means MOST NEARLY
    A. rashness
    B. caution
    C. without fear
    D. immunity

13. In the sentence, *The new officer displayed unusual temerity during the emergency*, the word *temerity* means MOST NEARLY
    A. fear
    B. rashness
    C. calmness
    D. anxiety

14. In the sentence, *The portions of food were parsimoniously served*, the word *parsimoniously* means MOST NEARLY
    A. stingily
    B. piously
    C. elaborately
    D. generously

15. In the sentence, *Generally the speaker's remarks were sententious*, the word *sententious* means MOST NEARLY
    A. verbose
    B. witty
    C. argumentative
    D. pithy

Questions 16-20.

DIRECTIONS: Next to the number which corresponds with the number of each item in Column I, place the letter preceding the adjective in Column II which BEST describes the persons in Column I.

COLUMN I		COLUMN II
16. Talkative woman	A.	abstemious
17. Person on a reducing diet	B.	pompous
18. Scholarly professor	C.	erudite
19. Man who seldom speaks	D.	benevolent
20. Charitable person	E.	docile
	F.	loquacious
	G.	indefatigable
	H.	taciturn

Questions 21-25.

DIRECTIONS: Next to the number which corresponds with the number preceding each profession in Column I, place the letter preceding the word in Column II which BEST explains the subject matter of that profession.

COLUMN I		COLUMN II	
21.	Geologist	A.	animals
22.	Oculist	B.	eyes
23.	Podiatrist	C.	feet
24.	Palmist	D.	fortune-telling
25.	Zoologist	E.	language
		F.	rocks
		G.	stamps
		H.	woman

Questions 26-30.

DIRECTIONS: Next to the number corresponding to the number of each of the words in Column I, place the letter preceding the word in Column II that is MOST NEARLY OPPOSITE to it in meaning.

COLUMN I		COLUMN II	
26.	comely	A.	beautiful
27.	eminent	B.	cowardly
28.	frugal	C.	kind
29.	gullible	D.	sedate
30.	valiant	E.	shrewd
		F.	ugly
		G.	unknown
		H.	wasteful

KEY (CORRECT ANSWERS)

1.	C	11.	A	21.	F
2.	A	12.	D	22.	B
3.	B	13.	B	23.	C
4.	B	14.	A	24.	D
5.	C	15.	D	25.	A
6.	B	16.	F	26.	F
7.	B	17.	A	27.	G
8.	A	18.	C	28.	H
9.	B	19.	H	29.	E
10.	C	20.	D	30.	B

PREPARING WRITTEN MATERIALS

EXAMINATION SECTION
TEST 1

DIRECTIONS: Each of the two sentences in the following questions may contain errors in punctuation, capitalization, or grammar.
If there is an error in only Sentence I, mark your answer A. If there is an error in only Sentence II, mark your answer B.
If there is an error in both Sentence I and Sentence II, mark your answer C. If both Sentence I and II are correct, mark your answer D.
PRINT THE LETTER OF THE CORRECT ANSWER IN THE SPACE AT THE RIGHT.

1. I. The task of typing these reports is to be divided equally between you and me.   1.____
   II. If it was he, I would use a different method for filing these records.

2. I. The new clerk is just as capable as some of the older employees, if not more capable.   2.____
   II. Using his knowledge of arithmetic to check the calculation, the supervisor found no errors in the report.

3. I. A typist who does consistently superior work probably merits promotion.   3.____
   II. In its report on the stenographic unit, the committee pointed out that neither the stenographers nor the typists were adequately trained.

4. I. Entering the office, the desk was noticed immediately by the visitor.   4.____
   II. Arrangements have been made to give this training to whoever applies for it.

5. I. The office manager estimates that this assignment, which is to be handled by you and I, will require about two weeks for completion.   5.____
   II. One of the recommendations of the report is that these kind of forms be discarded because they are of no value.

6. I. The supervisor knew that the typist was a quiet, cooperative, efficient, employee.   6.____
   II. The duties of stenographer are to take dictation notes at conferences and transcribing them.

7. I. The stenographer has learned that she, as well as two typists, is being assigned to the new unit.   7.____
   II. We do not know who you have designated to take charge of the new program.

8. I. He asked, "When do you expect to return?"   8.____
   II. I doubt whether this system will be successful here; it is not suitable for the work of our agency.

9. I. It is a policy of this agency to encourage punctuality as a good habit for we employees to adopt.
   II. The successful completion of the task was due largely to them cooperating effectively with the supervisor.

9.____

10. I. Mr. Smith, who is a very competent executive has offered his services to our department.
    II. Every one of the stenographers who work in this office is considered trustworthy.

10.____

11. I. It is very annoying to have a pencil sharpener, which is not in proper working order.
    II. The building watchman checked the door of Charlie's office and found that the lock has been jammed.

11.____

12. I. Since he went on the New York City council a year ago, one of his primary concerns has been safety in the streets.
    II. After waiting in the doorway for about 15 minutes, a black sedan appeared.

12.____

13. I. When you are studying a good textbook is important.
    II. He said he would divide the money equally between you and me.

13.____

14. I. The question is, "How can a large number of envelopes be sealed rapidly without the use of sealing machine?"
    II. The administrator assigned two stenographers, Mary and I, to the new bureau.

14.____

15. I. A dictionary, in addition to the office management textbooks, were placed on his desk.
    II. The concensus of opinion is that none of the employees should be required to work overtime.

15.____

16. I. Mr. Granger has demonstrated that he is as courageous, if not more courageous, than Mr. Brown.
    II. The successful completion of the project depends on the manager's accepting our advisory opinion.

16.____

17. I. Mr. Ames was in favor of issuing a set of rules and regulations for all of us employees to follow.
    II. It is inconceivable that the new clerk knows how to deal with that kind of correspondence.

17.____

18. I. The revised referrence manual is to be used by all of the employees.
    II. Mr. Johnson told Miss Kent and me to accumulate all the letters that we receive.

18.____

19. I. The supervisor said, that before any changes would be made in the attendance report, there must be ample justification for them.
    II. Each of them was asked to amend their preliminary report.

19.____

20. I. Mrs. Peters conferred with Mr. Roberts before she laid the papers on his desk.
    II. As far as this report is concerned, Mr. Williams always has and will be responsible for its preparation.

20.____

KEY (CORRECT ANSWERS)

1.	B	11.	C
2.	D	12.	C
3.	D	13.	A
4.	A	14.	B
5.	C	15.	C
6.	C	16.	A
7.	B	17.	B
8.	D	18.	A
9.	C	19.	C
10.	A	20.	B

TEST 2

DIRECTIONS: Each question or incomplete statement is followed by several suggested answers or completions. Select the one that BEST answers the question or completes the statement. *PRINT THE LETTER OF THE CORRECT ANSWER IN THE SPACE AT THE RIGHT.*

Questions 1-9.

DIRECTIONS: Questions 1 through 9 consist of pairs of sentences which may or may not contain errors in grammar, capitalization, or punctuation.
If both sentences are correct, mark your answer A.
If the first sentence only is correct, mark your answer B.
If the second sentence only is correct, mark your answer C.
If both sentences are incorrect, mark your answer D.
NOTE: Consider a sentence correct if it contains no errors, although there may be other correct ways of writing the sentence.

1. I. An unusual conference will be held today at George Washington high school. 1.____
   II. The principal of the school, Dr. Pace, described the meeting as "a unique opportunity for educators to exchange ideas.

2. I. Studio D, which they would ordinarily use, will be occupied at that time. 2.____
   II. Any other studio, which is properly equipped, may be used instead.

3. I. D.H. Lawrence's <u>Sons and Lovers</u> were discussed on today's program. 3.____
   II. Either Eliot's or Yeats's work is to be covered next week.

4. I. This program is on the air for three years now, and has a well-established audience. 4.____
   II. We have received many complimentary letters from listeners, and scarcely no critical ones.

5. I. Both Mr. Owen and Mr. Mitchell have addressed the group. 5.____
   II. As has Mr. Stone, whose talks have been especially well received.

6. I. The original program was different in several respects from the version that eventually went on the air. 6.____
   II. Each of the three announcers who Mr. Scott thought had had suitable experience was asked whether he would be willing to take on the special assignment.

7. I. A municipal broadcasting system provides extensive coverage of local events, but also reports national and international news. 7.____
   II. A detailed account of happenings in the South may be carried by a local station hundreds of miles away.

8. I. Jack Doe the announcer and I will be working on the program. 8.____
   II. The choice of musical selections has been left up to he and I.

64

9. I. Mr. Taylor assured us that "he did not anticipate any difficulty in making arrangements for the broadcast."
    II. Although there had seemed at first to be certain problems; these had been solved.

Questions 10-14.

DIRECTIONS: Questions 10 through 14 consist of pairs of sentences which may contain errors in grammar, sentence structure, punctuation, or spelling, or both sentences may be correct. Consider a sentence correct if it contains no errors, although there may be other correct ways of writing the sentence.
If only Sentence I contains an error, mark your answer A.
If only Sentence II contains an error, mark your answer B.
If both sentences contain errors, mark your answer C.
If both sentences are correct, mark your answer D.

10. I. No employee considered to be indispensable will be assigned to the new office.
    II. The arrangement of the desks and chairs give the office a neat appearance.

11. I. The recommendation, accompanied by a report, was delivered this morning.
    II. Mr. Green thought the procedure would facilitate his work; he knows better now.

12. I. Limiting the term "property" to tangible property, in the criminal mischief setting, accords with prior case law holding that only tangible property came within the purview of the offense of malicious mischief.
    II. Thus, a person who intentionally destroys the property of another, but under an honest belief that he has title to such property, cannot be convicted of criminal mischief under the Revised Penal Law.

13. I. Very early in its history, New York enacted statutes from time to time punishing, either as a felony or as a misdemeanor, malicious injuries to various kinds of property: piers, booms, dams, bridges, etc.
    II. The application of the statute is necessarily restricted to trespassory takings with larcenous intent: namely with intent permanently or virtually permanently to "appropriate" property or "deprive" the owner of its use.

14. I. Since the former Penal Law did not define the instruments of forgery in a general fashion, its crime of forgery was held to be narrower than the common law offense in this respect and to embrace only those instruments explicitly specified in the substantive provisions.
    II. After entering the barn through an open door for the purpose of stealing, it was closed by the defendants.

Questions 15-20.

DIRECTIONS: Questions 15 through 20 consist of pairs of sentences which may or may not contain errors in grammar, capitalization, or punctuation.
If both sentences are correct, mark your answer A.
If the first sentence only is correct, mark your answer B.
If the second sentence only is correct, mark your answer C.
If both sentences are incorrect, mark your answer D.
NOTE: Consider a sentence correct if it contains no errors, although there may be other ways of writing the sentence.

15. I. The program, which is currently most popular, is a news broadcast. 15.____
    II. The engineer assured his supervisor that there was no question of his being late again.

16. I. The announcer recommended that the program originally scheduled for that time be cancelled. 16.____
    II. Copies of the script may be given to whoever is interested.

17. I. A few months ago it looked like we would be able to broadcast the concert live. 17.____
    II. The program manager, as well as the announcers, were enthusiastic about the plan.

18. I. No speaker on the subject of education is more interesting than he. 18.____
    II. If he would have had the time, we would have scheduled him for a regular weekly broadcast.

19. I. This quartet, in its increasingly complex variations on a simple theme, admirably illustrates Professor Baker's point. 19.____
    II. Listeners interested in these kind of ideas will find his recently published study of Haydn rewarding.

20. I. The Commissioner's resignation at the end of next month marks the end of a long public service career. 20.____
    II. Outstanding among his numerous achievements were his successful implementation of several revolutionary schemes to reorganize the agency.

KEY (CORRECT ANSWERS)

1.	C	11.	D
2.	B	12.	C
3.	C	13.	B
4.	D	14.	A
5.	B	15.	C
6.	A	16.	A
7.	A	17.	D
8.	D	18.	B
9.	D	19.	B
10.	B	20.	B

PREPARING WRITTEN MATERIAL
EXAMINATION SECTION
TEST 1

DIRECTIONS: Each question or incomplete statement is followed by several suggested answers or completions. Select the one that BEST answers the question or completes the statement. *PRINT THE LETTER OF THE CORRECT ANSWER IN THE SPACE AT THE RIGHT.*

1. The one of the following sentences which is LEAST acceptable from the viewpoint of correct usage is:
   A. The police thought the fugitive to be him.
   B. The criminals set a trap for whoever would fall into it.
   C. It is ten years ago since the fugitive fled from the city.
   D. The lecturer argued that criminals are usually cowards.
   E. The police removed four bucketfuls of earth from the scene of the crime.

1.____

2. The one of the following sentences which is LEAST acceptable from the viewpoint of correct usage is:
   A. The patrolman scrutinized the report with great care.
   B. Approaching the victim of the assault, two bruises were noticed by the patrolman.
   C. As soon as I had broken down the door, I stepped into the room.
   D. I observed the accused loitering near the building, which was closed at the time.
   E. The storekeeper complained that his neighbor was guilty of violating a local ordinance.

2.____

3. The one of the following sentences which is LEAST acceptable from the viewpoint of correct usage is:
   A. I realized immediately that he intended to assault the woman, so I disarmed him.
   B. It was apparent that Mr. Smith's explanation contained many inconsistencies.
   C. Despite the slippery condition of the street, he managed to stop the vehicle before injuring the child.
   D. Not a single one of them wish, despite the damage to property, to make a formal complaint.
   E. The body was found lying on the floor.

3.____

4. The one of the following sentences which contains NO error in usage is:
   A. After the robbers left, the proprietor stood tied in his chair for about two hours before help arrived.
   B. In the cellar I found the watchman's hat and coat.
   C. The persons living in adjacent apartments stated that they had heard no unusual noises.

4.____

D. Neither a knife or any firearms were found in the room.
E. Walking down the street, the shouting of the crowd indicated that something was wrong.

5. The one of the following sentences which contains NO error in usage is:
    A. The policeman lay a firm hand on the suspect's shoulder.
    B. It is true that neither strength nor agility are the most important requirement for a good patrolman.
    C. Good citizens constantly strive to do more than merely comply the restraints imposed by society.
    D. No decision was made as to whom the prize should be awarded.
    E. Twenty years is considered a severe sentence for a felony.

6. Which of the following sentences is NOT expressed in standard English usage?
    A. The victim reached a pay-phone booth and manages to call police headquarters.
    B. By the time the call was received, the assailant had left the scene.
    C. The victim has been a respected member of the community for the past eleven years.
    D. Although the lighting was bad and the shadows were deep, the storekeeper caught sight of the attacker.
    E. Additional street lights have since been installed, and the patrols have been strengthened.

7. Which of the following sentences is NOT expressed in standard English usage?
    A. The judge upheld the attorney's right to question the witness about the missing glove.
    B. To be absolutely fair to all parties is the jury's chief responsibility.
    C. Having finished the report, a loud noise in the next room startled the sergeant.
    D. The witness obviously enjoyed having played a part in the proceedings.
    E. The sergeant planned to assign the case to whoever arrived first.

8. In which of the following sentences is a word misused?
    A. As a matter of principle, the captain insisted that the suspect's partner be brought for questioning.
    B. The principle suspect had been detained at the station house for most of the day.
    C. The principal in the crime had no previous criminal record, but his closest associate had been convicted of felonies on two occasions.
    D. The interest payments had been made promptly, but the firm had been drawing upon the principal for these payments.
    E. The accused insisted that his high school principal would furnish him a character reference.

9. Which of the following statements is ambiguous?
   A. Mr. Sullivan explained why Mr. Johnson had been dismissed from his job.
   B. The storekeeper told the patrolman he had made a mistake.
   C. After waiting three hours, the patients in the doctor's office were sent home.
   D. The janitor's duties were to maintain the building in good shape and to answer tenants' complaints.
   E. The speed limit should, in my opinion, be raised to sixty miles an hour on that stretch of road.

10. In which of the following is the punctuation or capitalization faulty?
    A. The accident occurred at an intersection in the Kew Gardens section of Queens, near the bus stop.
    B. The sedan, not the convertible, was struck in the side.
    C. Before any of the patrolmen had left the police car received an important message from headquarters.
    D. The dog that had been stolen was returned to his master, John Dempsey, who lived in East Village.
    E. The letter had been sent to 12 Hillside Terrace, Rutland, Vermont 05702.

Questions 11-25.

DIRECTIONS: Questions 11 through 25 are to be answered in accordance with correct English usage; that is, standard English rather than nonstandard or substandard. Nonstandard and substandard English includes words or expressions usually classified as slang, dialect, illiterate, etc., which are not generally accepted as correct in current written communication. Standard English also requires clarity, proper punctuation and capitalization and appropriate use of words. Write the letter of the sentence NOT expressed in standard English usage in the space at the right.

11. A. There were three witnesses to the accident.
    B. At least three witnesses were found to testify for the plaintiff.
    C. Three of the witnesses who took the stand was uncertain about the defendant's competence to drive.
    D. Only three witnesses came forward to testify for the plaintiff.
    E. The three witnesses to the accident were pedestrians.

12. A. The driver had obviously drunk too many martinis before leaving for home.
    B. The boy who drowned had swum in these same waters many times before.
    C. The petty thief had stolen a bicycle from a private driveway before he was apprehended.
    D. The detectives had brung in the heroin shipment they intercepted.
    E. The passengers had never ridden in a converted bus before.

13. A. Between you and me, the new platoon plan sounds like a good idea.
     B. Money from an aunt's estate was left to his wife and he.
     C. He and I were assigned to the same patrol for the first time in two months.
     D. Either you or he should check the front door of that store.
     E. The captain himself was not sure of the witness's reliability.

14. A. The alarm had scarcely begun to ring when the explosion occurred.
     B. Before the firemen arrived at the scene, the second story had been destroyed.
     C. Because of the dense smoke and heat, the firemen could hardly approach the now-blazing structure.
     D. According to the patrolman's report, there wasn't nobody in the store when the explosion occurred.
     E. The sergeant's suggestion was not at all unsound, but no one agreed with him.

15. A. The driver and the passenger they were both found to be intoxicated.
     B. The driver and the passenger talked slowly and not too clearly.
     C. Neither the driver nor his passengers were able to give a coherent account of the accident.
     D. In a corner of the room sat the passenger, quietly dozing.
     E. the driver finally told a strange and unbelievable story, which the passenger contradicted.

16. A. Under the circumstances I decided not to continue my examination of the premises.
     B. There are many difficulties now not comparable with those existing in 1960.
     C. Friends of the accused were heard to announce that the witness had better been away on the day of the trial.
     D. The two criminals escaped in the confusion that followed the explosion.
     E. The aged man was struck by the considerateness of the patrolman's offer.

17. A. An assemblage of miscellaneous weapons lay on the table.
     B. Ample opportunities were given to the defendant to obtain counsel.
     C. The speaker often alluded to his past experience with youthful offenders in the armed forces.
     D. The sudden appearance of the truck aroused my suspicions.
     E. Her studying had a good affect on her grades in high school.

18. A. He sat down in the theater and began to watch the movie.
     B. The girl had ridden horses since she was four years old.
     C. Application was made on behalf of the prosecutor to cite the witness for contempt.
     D. The bank robber, with his two accomplices, were caught in the act.
     E. His story is simply not credible.

19. A. The angry boy said that he did not like those kind of friends.
     B. The merchant's financial condition was so precarious that he felt he must avail himself of any offer of assistance.
     C. He is apt to promise more than he can perform.
     D. Looking at the messy kitchen, the housewife felt like crying.
     E. A clerk was left in charge of the stolen property.

20. A. His wounds were aggravated by prolonged exposure to sub-freezing temperatures.
     B. The prosecutor remarked that the witness was not averse to changing his story each time he was interviewed.
     C. The crime pattern indicated that the burglars were adapt in the handling of explosives.
     D. His rigid adherence to a fixed plan brought him into renewed conflict with his subordinates.
     E. He had anticipated that the sentence would be delivered by noon.

21. A. The whole arraignment procedure is badly in need of revision.
     B. After his glasses were broken in the fight, he would of gone to the optometrist if he could.
     C. Neither Tom nor Jack brought his lunch to work.
     D. He stood aside until the quarrel was over.
     E. A statement in the psychiatrist's report disclosed that the probationer vowed to have his revenge.

22. A. His fiery and intemperate speech to the striking employees fatally affected any chance of a future reconciliation.
     B. The wording of the statute has been variously construed.
     C. The defendant's attorney, speaking in the courtroom, called the official a demagogue who contempuously disregarded the judge's orders.
     D. The baseball game is likely to be the most exciting one this year.
     E. The mother divided the cookies among her two children.

23. A. There was only a bed and a dresser in the dingy room.
     B. John was one of the few students that have protested the new rule.
     C. It cannot be argued that the child's testimony is negligible; it is, on the contrary, of the greatest importance.
     D. The basic criterion for clearance was so general that officials resolved any doubts in favor of dismissal.
     E. Having just returned from a long vacation, the officer found the city unbearably hot.

24. A. The librarian ought to give more help to small children.
     B. The small boy was criticized by the teacher because he often wrote careless.
     C. It was generally doubted whether the women would permit the use of her apartment for intelligence operations.
     D. The probationer acts differently every time the officer visits him.
     E. Each of the newly appointed officers has 12 years of service.

25.
- A. The North is the most industrialized region in the country.
- B. L. Patrick Gray 3d, the bureau's acting director, stated that, while "rehabilitation is fine" for some convicted criminals, "it is a useless gesture for those who resist every such effort."
- C. Careless driving, faulty mechanism, narrow or badly kept roads all play their part in causing accidents.
- D. The childrens' books were left in the bus.
- E. It was a matter of internal security; consequently, he felt no inclination to rescind his previous order.

25.____

KEY (CORRECT ANSWERS)

1. C
2. B
3. D
4. C
5. E

6. A
7. C
8. B
9. B
10. C

11. C
12. D
13. B
14. D
15. A

16. C
17. E
18. D
19. A
20. C

21. B
22. E
23. B
24. B
25. D

TEST 2

DIRECTIONS: Each question or incomplete statement is followed by several suggested answers or completions. Select the one that BEST answers the question or completes the statement. *PRINT THE LETTER OF THE CORRECT ANSWER IN THE SPACE AT THE RIGHT.*

Questions 1-6.

DIRECTIONS: Each of Questions 1 through 6 consists of a statement which contains a word (one of those underlined) that is either incorrectly used because it is not in keeping with the meaning the quotation is evidently intended to convey, or is misspelled. There is only one INCORRECT word in each quotation. Of the four underlined words, determine if the first one should be replaced by the word lettered A, the second replaced by the word lettered B, the third replaced by the word lettered C, or the fourth replaced by the word lettered D.

1. Whether one depends on fluorescent or artificial light or both, adequate standards should be maintained by means of systematic tests.
   A. natural   B. safeguards   C. established   D. routine   1.____

2. A police officer has to be prepared to assume his knowledge as a social scientist in the community.
   A. forced   B. role   C. philosopher   D. street   2.____

3. It is practically impossible to indicate whether a sentence is too long simply by measuring its length.
   A. almost   B. tell   C. very   D. guessing   3.____

4. Strong leaders are required to organize a community for delinquency prevention and for dissemination of organized crime and drug addiction.
   A. tactics   B. important   C. control   D. meetings   4.____

5. The demonstrators who were taken to the Criminal Courts building in Manhattan (because it was large enough to accommodate them), contended that the arrests were unwarranted.
   A. demonstraters   B. Manhatten
   C. accomodate   D. unwarranted   5.____

6. They were guaranteed a calm atmosphere, free from harassment, which would be conducive to quiet consideration of the indictments.
   A. guarenteed   B. atmspher
   C. harassment   D. inditements   6.____

Questions 7-11.

DIRECTIONS: Each of Questions 7 through 11 consists of a statement containing four words in capital letters. One of these words in capital letters is not in keeping with the meaning which the statement is evidently intended to carry. The four words in capital letters in each statement are reprinted after the statement. Print the capital letter preceding the one of the four words which does MOST to spoil the true meaning of the statement in the space at the right.

7. Retirement and pension systems are essential not only to provide employees with with a means of support in the future, but also to prevent longevity and CHARITABLE considerations from UPSETTING the PROMOTIONAL opportunities RETIRED members of the career service. 7.____
   A. charitable   B. upsetting   C. promotional   D. retired

8. Within each major DIVISION in a properly set up public or private organization, provision is made so that each NECESSARY activity is CARED for and lines of authority and responsibility are clear-cut and INFINITE. 8.____
   A. division   B. necessary   C. cared   D. infinite

9. In public service, the scale of salaries paid must be INCIDENTAL to the services rendered, with due CONSIDERATION for the attraction of the desired MANPOWER and for the maintenance of a standard of living COMMENSURATE with the work to be performed. 9.____
   A. incidental   B. consideration
   C. manpower   D. commensurate

10. An understanding of the AIMS of an organization by the staff will AID greatly in increasing the DEMAND of the correspondence work of the office, and will to a large extent DETERMINE the nature of the correspondence. 10.____
    A. aims   B. aid   C. demand   D. determine

11. BECAUSE the Civil Service Commission strongly feels that the MERIT system is a key factor in the MAINTENANCE of democratic government, it has adopted as one of its major DEFENSES the progressive democratization of its own procedures in dealing with candidates for positions in the public service. 11.____
    A. Because   B. merit   C. maintenance   D. defenses

Questions 12-14.

DIRECTIONS: Questions 12 through 14 consist of one sentence each. Each sentence contains an incorrectly used word. First, decide which is the incorrectly used word. Then, from among the options given, decide which word, when substituted for the incorrectly used word, makes the meaning of the sentence clear.
EXAMPLE:
The U.S. national income exhibits a pattern of long term deflection.
   A. reflection   B. subjection   C. rejoicing   D. growth

The word *deflection* in the sentence does not convey the meaning the sentence evidently intended to convey. The word *growth* (Answer D), when substituted for the word *deflection*, makes the meaning of the sentence clear. Accordingly, the answer to the question is D.

12. The study commissioned by the joint committee fell compassionately short of the mark and would have to be redone.
    A. successfully   B. insignificantly
    C. experimentally   D. woefully

13. He will not idly exploit any violation of the provisions of the order.
    A. tolerate   B. refuse   C. construe   D. guard

14. The defendant refused to be virile and bitterly protested service.
    A. irked   B. feasible   C. docile   D. credible

Questions 15-25.

DIRECTIONS: Questions 15 through 25 consist of short paragraphs. Each paragraph contains one word which is INCORRECTLY used because it is NOT in keeping with the meaning of the paragraph. Find the word in each paragraph which is INCORRECTLY used and then select as the answer the suggested word which should be substituted for the incorrectly used word.

SAMPLE QUESTION:
In determining who is to do the work in your unit, you will have to decide just who does what from day to day. One of your lowest responsibilities is to assign work so that everybody gets a fair share and that everyone can do his part well.
    A. new   B. old   C. important   D. performance

EXPLANATION:
The word which is NOT in keeping with the meaning of the paragraph is *lowest*. This is the INCORRECTLY used word. The suggested word *important* would be in keeping with the meaning of the paragraph and should be substituted for *lowest*. Therefore, the CORRECT answer is choice C.

15. If really good practice in the elimination of preventable injuries is to be achieved and held in any establishment, top management must refuse full and definite responsibility and must apply a good share of its attention to the task.
    A. accept   B. avoidable   C. duties   D. problem

16. Recording the human face for identification is by no means the only service performed by the camera in the field of investigation. When the trial of any issue takes place, a word picture is sought to be distorted to the court of incidents, occurrences, or events which are in dispute.
    A. appeals   B. description   C. portrayed   D. deranged

4 (#2)

17. In the collection of physical evidence, it cannot be emphasized too strongly that a haphazard systematic search at the scene of the crime is vital. Nothing must be overlooked. Often the only leads in a case will come from the results of this search.
    A. important
    B. investigation
    C. proof
    D. thorough

17._____

18. If an investigator has reason to suspect that the witness is mentally stable, or a habitual drunkard, he should leave no stone unturned in his investigation to determine if the witness was under the influence of liquor or drugs, or was mentally unbalanced either at the time of the occurrence to which he testified or at the time of the trial.
    A. accused   B. clue   C. deranged   D. question

18._____

19. The use of records is a valuable step in crime investigation and is the main reason every department should maintain accurate reports. Crimes are not committed through the use of departmental records alone but from the use of all records, of almost every type, wherever they may be found and whenever they give any incidental information regarding the criminal.
    A. accidental   B. necessary   C. reported   D. solved

19._____

20. In the years since passage of the Harrison Narcotic Act of 1914, making the possession of opium amphetamines illegal in most circumstances, drug use has become a subject of considerable scientific interest and investigation. There is at present a voluminous literature on drug use of various kinds.
    A. ingestion   B. derivatives   C. addiction   D. opiates

20._____

21. Of course, the fact that criminal laws are extremely patterned in definition does not mean that the majority of persons who violate them are dealt with as criminals. Quite the contrary, for a great many forbidden acts are voluntarily engaged in within situations of privacy and go unobserved and unreported.
    A. symbolic   B. casual   C. scientific   D. broad-gauged

21._____

22. The most punitive way to study punishment is to focus attention on the pattern of punitive action: to study how a penalty is applied, too study what is done to or taken from an offender.
    A. characteristic   B. degrading   C. objective   D. distinguished

22._____

23. The most common forms of punishment in times past have been death, physical torture, mutilation, branding, public humiliation, fines, forfeits of property, banishment, transportation, and imprisonment. Although this list is by no means differentiated, practically every form of punishment has had several variations and applications.
    A. specific   B. simple   C. exhaustive   D. characteristic

23._____

24. There is another important line of inference between ordinary and professional criminals, and that is the source from which they are recruited. The professional criminal seems to be drawn from legitimate employment and, in many instances, from parallel vocations or pursuits.
   A. demarcation   B. justification   C. superiority   D. reference

24.____

25. He took the position that the success of the program was insidious on getting additional revenue.
   A. reputed   B. contingent   C. failure   D. indeterminate

25.____

KEY (CORRECT ANSWERS)

1.	A	11.	D
2.	B	12.	D
3.	B	13.	A
4.	C	14.	C
5.	D	15.	A
6.	C	16.	C
7.	D	17.	D
8.	D	18.	C
9.	A	19.	D
10.	C	20.	B

21.	D
22.	C
23.	C
24.	A
25.	B

TEST 3

DIRECTIONS: Each question or incomplete statement is followed by several suggested answers or completions. Select the one that BEST answers the question or completes the statement. *PRINT THE LETTER OF THE CORRECT ANSWER IN THE SPACE AT THE RIGHT.*

Questions 1-5.

DIRECTIONS: Questions 1 through 5 are to be answered on the basis of the following.

You are a supervising officer in an investigative unit. Earlier in the day, you directed Detectives Tom Dixon and Sal Mayo to investigate a reported assault and robbery in a liquor store within your area of jurisdiction.

Detective Dixon has submitted to you a preliminary investigative report containing the following information:

- At 1630 hours on 2/20, arrived at Joe's Liquor Store at 350 SW Avenue with Detective Mayo to investigate A & R.
- At store interviewed Rob Ladd, store manager, who stated that he and Joe Brown (store owner) had been stuck up about ten minutes prior to our arrival.
- Ladd described the robbers as male whites in their late teens or early twenties. Further stated that one of the robbers displayed what appeared to be an automatic pistol as he entered the store, and said, *Give us the money or we'll kill you.* Ladd stated that Brown then reached under the counter where he kept a loaded .38 caliber pistol. Several shots followed, and Ladd threw himself to the floor.
- The robbers fled, and Ladd didn't know if any money had been taken.
- At this point, Ladd realized that Brown was unconscious on the floor and bleeding from a head wound.
- Ambulance called by Ladd, and Brown was removed by same to General Hospital.
- Personally interviewed John White, 382 Dartmouth Place, who stated he was inside store at the time of occurrence. White states that he hid behind a wine display upon hearing someone say, *Give us the money.* He then heard shots and saw two young men run from the store to a yellow car parked at the curb. White was unable to further describe auto. States the taller of the two men drove the car away while the other sat on passenger side in front.
- Recovered three spent .38 caliber bullets from premises and delivered them to Crime Lab.
- To General Hospital at 1800 hours but unable to interview Brown, who was under sedation and suffering from shock and a laceration of the head.
- Alarm #12487 transmitted for car and occupants.
- Case Active.

Based solely on the contents of the preliminary investigation submitted by Detective Dixon, select one sentence from the following groups of sentences which is MOST accurate and is grammatically correct.

1. A. Both robbers were armed.
    B. Each of the robbers were described as a male white.
    C. Neither robber was armed.
    D. Mr. Ladd stated that one of the robbers was armed.

    1.____

2. A. Mr. Brown fired three shots from his revolver.
    B. Mr. Brown was shot in the head by one of the robbers.
    C. Mr. Brown suffered a gunshot wound of the head during the course of the robbery.
    D. Mr. Brown was taken to General Hospital by ambulance.

    2.____

3. A. Shots were fired after one of the robbers said, *Give us the money or we'll kill you.*
    B. After one of the robbers demanded the money from Mr. Brown, he fired a shot.
    C. The preliminary investigation indicated that although Mr. Brown did not have a license for the gun, he was justified in using deadly physical force.
    D. Mr. Brown was interviewed at General Hospital.

    3.____

4. A. Each of the witnesses were customers in the store at the time of occurrence.
    B. Neither of the witnesses interviewed was the owner of the liquor store.
    C. Neither of the witnesses interviewed were the owner of the store.
    D. Neither of the witnesses was employed by Mr. Brown.

    4.____

5. A. Mr. Brown arrived at General Hospital at about 5:00 P.M.
    B. Neither of the robbers was injured during the robbery.
    C. The robbery occurred at 3:30 P.M. on February 10.
    D. One of the witnesses called the ambulance.

    5.____

Questions 6-10.

DIRECTIONS: Each of Questions 6 through 10 consists of information given in outline form and four sentences labeled A, B, C, and D. For each question, choose the one sentence which CORRECTLY expresses the information given in outline form and which also displays PROPER English usage.

6. Client's Name: Joanna Jones
    Number of Children: 3
    Client's Income: None
    Client's Marital Status: Single

    A. Joanna Jones is an unmarried client with three children who have no income.
    B. Joanna Jones, who is single and has no income, a client she has three children.
    C. Joanna Jones, whose three children are clients, is single and has no income.
    D. Joanna Jones, who has three children, is an unmarried client with no income.

    6.____

7. Client's Name: Bertha Smith
   Number of Children: 2
   Client's Rent: $1050 per month
   Number of Rooms: 4

   A. Bertha Smith, a client, pays $1050 per month for her four rooms with two children.
   B. Client Bertha Smith has two children and pays $1050 per month for four rooms.
   C. Client Bertha Smith is paying $1050 per month for two children with four rooms.
   D. For four rooms and two children client Bertha Smith pays $1050 per month.

7.____

8. Name of Employee: Cynthia Dawes
   Number of Cases Assigned: 9
   Date Cases were Assigned: 12/16
   Number of Assigned Cases Completed: 8

   A. On December 16, employee Cynthia Dawes was assigned nine cases; she has completed eight of these cases.
   B. Cynthia Dawes, employee on December 16, assigned nine cases, completed eight.
   C. Being employed on December 16, Cynthia Dawes completed eight of nine assigned cases.
   D. Employee Cynthia Dawes, she was assigned nine cases and completed eight, on December 16.

8.____

9. Place of Audit: Broadway Center
   Names of Auditors: Paul Cahn, Raymond Perez
   Date of Audit: 11/20
   Number of Cases Audited: 41

   A. On November 20, at the Broadway Center 41 cases was audited by auditors Paul Cahn and Raymond Perez.
   B. Auditors Raymond Perez and Paul Cahn has audited 41 cases at the Broadway Center on November 20.
   C. At the Broadway Center, on November 20, auditors Paul Cahn and Raymond Perez audited 41 cases.
   D. Auditors Paul Cahn and Raymond Perez at the Broadway Center, on November 20, is auditing 41 cases.

9.____

10. Name of Client: Barbra Levine
    Client's Monthly Income: $2100
    Client's Monthly Expenses: $4520

    A. Barbra Levine is a client, her monthly income is $2100 and her monthly expenses is $4520.
    B. Barbra Levine's monthly income is $2100 and she is a client, with whose monthly expenses are $4520.

10.____

C. Barbra Levine is a client whose monthly income is $2100 and whose monthly expenses are $4520.
D. Barbra Levine, a client, is with a monthly income which is $2100 and monthly expenses which are $4520.

Questions 11-13.

DIRECTIONS: Questions 11 through 13 involve several statements of fact presented in a very simple way. These statements of fact are followed by 4 choices which attempt to incorporate all of the facts into one logical statement which is properly constructed and grammatically correct.

11.
   I. Mr. Brown was sweeping the sidewalk in front of his house.
   II. He was sweeping it because it was dirty.
   III. He swept the refuse into the street.
   IV. Police Officer gave him a ticket.

   Which one of the following BEST presents the information given above?
   A. Because his sidewalk was dirty, Mr. Brown received a ticket from Officer Green when he swept the refuse into the street.
   B. Police Officer Green gave Mr. Brown a ticket because his sidewalk was dirty and he swept the refuse into the street.
   C. Police Officer Green gave Mr. Brown a ticket for sweeping refuse into the street because his sidewalk was dirty.
   D. Mr. Brown, who was sweeping refuse from his dirty sidewalk into the street, was given a ticket by Police Officer Green.

12.
   I. Sergeant Smith radioed for help.
   II. The sergeant did so because the crowd was getting larger.
   III. It was 10:00 A.M. when he made his call.
   IV. Sergeant Smith was not in uniform at the time of occurrence.

   Which one of the following BEST presents the information given above?
   A. Sergeant Smith, although not on duty at the time, radioed for help at 10 o'clock because the crowd was getting uglier.
   B. Although not in uniform, Sergeant Smith called for help at 10:00 A.M. because the crowd was getting uglier.
   C. Sergeant Smith radioed for help at 10:00 A.M. because the crowd was getting larger.
   D. Although he was not in uniform, Sergeant Smith radioed for help at 10:00 A.M. because the crowd was getting larger.

13.
   I. The payroll office is open on Fridays.
   II. Paychecks are distributed from 9:00 A.M. to 12 Noon.
   III. The office is open on Fridays because that's the only day the payroll staff is available.
   IV. It is open for the specified hours in order to permit employees to cash checks at the bank during lunch hour.

The choice below which MOST clearly and accurately presents the above idea is:
A. Because the payroll office is open on Fridays from 9:00 A.M. to 12 Noon, employees can cash their checks when the payroll staff is available.
B. Because the payroll staff is only available on Fridays until noon, employees can cash their checks during their lunch hour.
C. Because the payroll staff is available only on Fridays, the office is open from 9:00 A.M. to 12 Noon to allow employees to cash their checks.
D. Because of payroll staff availability, the payroll office is open on Fridays. It is open from 9:00 A.M. to 12 Noon so that distributed paychecks can be cashed at the bank while employees are on their lunch hour.

Questions 14-16.

DIRECTIONS: In each of Questions 14 through 6, the four sentences are from a paragraph in a report. They are not in the right order. Which of the following arrangements is the BEST one?

14. I. An executive may answer a letter by writing his reply on the face of the letter itself instead of having a return letter typed.
    II. This procedure is efficient because it saves the executive's time, the typist's time, and saves office file space.
    III. Copying machines are used in small offices as well as large offices to save time and money in making brief replies to business letters.
    IV. A copy is made on a copy machine to go into the company files, while the original is mailed back to the sender.

    The CORRECT answer is:
    A. I, II, IV, III   B. I, IV, II, III   C. III, I, IV, II   D. III, IV, II, I

14.____

15. I. Most organizations favor one of the types but always include the others to a lesser degree.
    II. However, we can detect a definite trend toward greater use of symbolic control.
    III. We suggest that our local police agencies are today primarily utilizing material control.
    IV. Control can be classified into three types: physical, material, and symbolic.

    The CORRECT answer is:
    A. IV, II, III, I   B. II, I, IV, III   C. III, IV, II, I   D. IV, I, III, II

15.____

16. I. They can and do take advantage of ancient political and geographical boundaries, which often give them sanctuary from effective policy activity.
    II. This country is essentially a country of small police forces, each operating independently within the limits of its jurisdiction.
    III. The boundaries that define and limit police operations do not hinder the movement of criminals, of course.
    IV. The machinery of law enforcement in America is fragmented, complicated, and frequently overlapping.

16.____

The CORRECT answer is:
A. III, I, IV   B. II, IV, I, III   C. IV, II, III, I   D. IV, III, II, I

17. Examine the following sentence, and then choose from below the words which should be inserted in the blank spaces to produce the best sentence.
The unit has exceeded _____ goals and the employees are satisfied with _____ accomplishments.
A. their, it's   B. it's; it's   C. its, there   D. its, their

18. Examine the following sentence, and then choose from below the words which should be inserted in the blank spaces to produce the best sentence.
Research indicates that employees who _____ no opportunity for close social relationships often find their work unsatisfying, and this _____ of satisfaction often reflects itself in low production.
A. have; lack   B. have; excess   C. has; lack   D. has; excess

19. Words in a sentence must be arranged properly to make sure that the intended meaning of the sentence is clear.
The sentence below that does NOT make sense because a clause has been separated from the word on which its meaning depends is:
A. To be a good writer, clarity is necessary.
B. To be a good writer, you must write clearly.
C. You must write clearly to be a good writer.
D. Clarity is necessary to good writing.

Questions 20-21.

DIRECTIONS: Each of Questions 20 and 21 consists of a statement which contains a word (one of those underlined) that is either incorrectly used because it is not in keeping with the meaning the quotation is evidently intended to convey, or is misspelled. There is only one INCORRECT word in each quotation. Of the four underlined words, determine if the first one should be replaced by the word lettered A, the second one replaced by the word lettered B, the third one replaced by the word lettered C, or the fourth one replaced by the word lettered D.

20. The alleged killer was occasionally permitted to excercise in the corridor.
A. alledged   B. ocasionally   C. permited   D. exercise

21. Defense counsel stated, in affect, that their conduct was permissible under the First Amendment.
A. council   B. effect   C. there   D. permissable

Question 22.

DIRECTIONS: Question 22 consists of one sentence. This sentence contains an incorrectly used word. First, decide which is the incorrectly used word. Then, from among the options given, decide which word, when substituted for the incorrectly used word, makes the meaning of the sentence clear.

22. As today's violence has no single cause, so its causes have no single scheme. 22.____
    A. deference   B. cure   C. flaw   D. relevance

23. In the sentence, *A man in a light-grey suit waited thirty-five minutes in the ante-room for the all-important document*, the word IMPROPERLY hyphenated is 23.____
    A. light-grey   B. thirty-five
    C. ante-room   D. all-important

24. In the sentence, *The candidate wants to file his application for preference before it is too late*, the word *before* is used as a(n) 24.____
    A. preposition   B. subordinating conjunction
    C. pronoun   D. adverb

25. In the sentence, *The perpetrators ran from the scene*, the word *from* is a 25.____
    A. preposition   B. pronoun   C. verb   D. conjunction

KEY (CORRECT ANSWERS)

1.	D	11.	D
2.	D	12.	D
3.	A	13.	D
4.	B	14.	C
5.	D	15.	D
6.	D	16.	C
7.	B	17.	D
8.	A	18.	A
9.	C	19.	A
10.	C	20.	D

21.	B
22.	B
23.	C
24.	B
25.	A

PREPARING WRITTEN MATERIAL

PARAGRAPH REARRANGEMENT
COMMENTARY

The sentences that follow are in scrambled order. You are to rearrange them in proper order and indicate the letter choice containing the correct answer at the space at the right.

Each group of sentences in this section is actually a paragraph presented in scrambled order. Each sentence in the group has a place in that paragraph; no sentence is to be left out. You are to read each group of sentences and decide upon the best order in which to put the sentences so as to form a well-organized paragraph.

The questions in this section measure the ability to solve a problem when all the facts relevant to its solution are not given.

More specifically, certain positions of responsibility and authority require the employee to discover connection between events sometimes, apparently, unrelated. In order to do this, the employee will find it necessary to correctly infer that unspecified events have probably occurred or are likely to occur. This ability becomes especially important when action must be taken on incomplete information.

Accordingly, these questions require competitors to choose among several suggested alternatives, each of which presents a different sequential arrangement of the events. Competitors must choose the MOST logical of the suggested sequences.

In order to do so, they may be required to draw on general knowledge to infer missing concepts or events that are essential to sequencing the given events. Competitors should be careful to infer only what is essential to the sequence. The plausibility of the wrong alternatives will always require the inclusion of unlikely events or of additional chains of events which are NOT essential to sequencing the given events.

It's very important to remember that you are looking for the best of the four possible choices, and that the best choice of all may not even be one of the answers you're given to choose from.

There is no one right way to solve these problems. Many people have found it helpful to first write out the order of the sentences, as they would have arranged them, on their scrap paper before looking at the possible answers. If their optimum answer is there, this can save them some time. If it isn't, this method can still give insight into solving the problem. Others find it most helpful to just go through each of the possible choices, contrasting each as they go along. You should use whatever method feels comfortable and works for you.

While most of these types of questions are not that difficult, we've added a higher percentage of the difficult type, just to give you more practice. Usually there are only one or two questions on this section that contain such subtle distinctions that you're unable to answer confidently. And you then may find yourself stuck deciding between two possible choices, neither of which you're sure about.

EXAMINATION SECTION

TEST 1

DIRECTIONS: The sentences that follow are in scrambled order. You are to rearrange them in proper order and indicate the letter choice containing the correct answer. *PRINT THE LETTER OF THE CORRECT ANSWER IN THE SPACE AT THE RIGHT.*

1. Below are four statements labeled W, X, Y and Z.
   W. He was a strict and fanatic drillmaster.
   X. The word is always used in a derogatory sense and generally shows resentment and anger on the part of the user.
   Y. It is from the name of this Frenchman that we derive our English word, martinet.
   Z. Jean Martinet was the Inspector-General of Infantry during the reign of King Louis XIV.
   The PROPER order in which these sentences should be placed in a paragraph is:
   A. X, Z, W, Y   B. X, Z, Y, W   C. Z, W, Y, X   D. Z, Y, W, X

1.____

2. In the following paragraph, the sentences, which are numbered, have been jumbled.
   I. Since then it has undergone changes.
   II. It was incorporated in 1955 under the laws of the State of New York.
   III. Its primary purposes, a cleaner city, has, however, remained the same.
   IV. The Citizens Committee works in cooperation with the Mayor's Inter-departmental Committee for a Clean City.
   The order in which these sentences should be arranged to form a well-organized paragraph is:
   A. II, IV, I, III   B. III, IV, I, II   C. IV, II, I, III   D. IV, III, II, I

2.____

3.____

Questions 3-5.

DIRECTIONS: The sentences listed below are part of a meaningful paragraph but they are not given in their proper order. You are to decide what would be the BEST order in which to put the sentences so as to form a well-organized paragraph. Each sentence has a place in the paragraph; there are no extra sentences. You are then to answer Questions 3 through 5 inclusive on the basis of your rearrangements of these scrambled sentences into a properly organized paragraph.

In 1887 some insurance companies organized an Inspection Department to advise their clients on all phases of fire prevention and protection. Probably this has been due to the smaller annual fire losses in Great Britain than in the United States. It tests various fire prevention devices and appliances and determines manufacturing hazards and their safeguards. Fire research began earlier in the United States and is more advanced than in Great Britain. Later they established a laboratory specializing in electrical, mechanical, hydraulic, and chemical fields.

3. When the five sentences are arranged in proper order, the paragraph starts with the sentence which begins
   A. "In 1887…"   B. "Probably this…"   C. "It tests…"
   D. "Fire research…"   E. "Later they…"

3.____

4. In the last sentence listed above, "they" refers to
   A. the insurance companies
   B. the United States and Great Britain
   C. the Inspection Department
   D. clients
   E. technicians

4.____

5. When the above paragraph is properly arranged, it ends with the words
   A. "…and protection."   B. "…the United States."
   C. "…their safeguards."   D. "…in Great Britain."
   E. "…chemical fields."

5.____

KEY (CORRECT ANSWERS)

1. C
2. C
3. D
4. A
5. C

TEST 2

DIRECTIONS: In each of the questions numbered I through V, several sentences are given. For each question, choose as your answer the group of number that represents the MOST logical order of these sentences if they were arranged in paragraph form. *PRINT THE LETTER OF THE CORRECT ANSWER IN THE SPACE AT THE RIGHT.*

1.
   I. It is established when one shows that the landlord has prevented the tenant's enjoyment of his interest in the property leased.
   II. Constructive eviction is the result of a breach of the covenant of quiet enjoyment implied in all leases.
   III. In some parts of the United States, it is not complete until the tenant vacates within a reasonable time.
   IV. Generally, the acts must be of such serious and permanent character as to deny the tenant the enjoyment of his possessing rights.
   V. In this event, upon abandonment of the premises, the tenant's liability for that ceases.
   The CORRECT answer is:
   A. II, I, IV, III, V
   B. V, II, III, I, IV
   C. IV, III, I, II, V
   D. I, III, V, IV, II

2.
   I. The powerlessness before private and public authorities that is the typical experience of the slum tenant is reminiscent of the situation of blue-collar workers all through the nineteenth century.
   II. Similarly, in recent years, this chapter of history has been reopened by anti-poverty groups which have attempted to organize slum tenants to enable them to bargain collectively with their landlords about the conditions of their tenancies.
   III. It is familiar history that many of the worker remedied their condition by joining together and presenting their demands collectively.
   IV. Like the workers, tenants are forced by the conditions of modern life into substantial dependence on these who possess great political aid and economic power.
   V. What's more, the very fact of dependence coupled with an absence of education and self-confidence makes them hesitant and unable to stand up for what they need from those in power.
   The CORRECT answer is:
   A. V, IV, I, II, III
   B. II, III, I, V, IV
   C. III, I, V, IV, II
   D. I, IV, V, III, II

3.
   I. A railroad, for example, when not acting as a common carrier may contract away responsibility for its own negligence.
   II. As to a landlord, however, no decision has been found relating to the legal effect of a clause shifting the statutory duty of repair to the tenant.
   III. The courts have not passed on the validity of clauses relieving the landlord of this duty and liability.
   IV. They have, however, upheld the validity of exculpatory clauses in other types of contracts.

91

V. Housing regulations impose a duty upon the landlord to maintain leased premises in safe condition.
VI. As another example, a bailee may limit his liability except for gross negligence, willful acts, or fraud.

The CORRECT answer is:
A. II, I, VI, IV, III, V
B. I, III, IV, V, VI, II
C. III, V, I, IV, II, VI
D. V, III, IV, I, VI, II

4.
I. Since there are only samples in the building, retail or consumer sales are generally eschewed by mart occupants, and in some instances, rigid controls are maintained to limit entrance to the mart only to those persons engaged in retailing.
II. Since World War I, in many larger cities, there has developed a new type of property, called the mart building.
III. It can, therefore, be used by wholesalers and jobbers for the display of sample merchandise.
IV. This type of building is most frequently a multi-storied, finished interior property which is a cross between a retail arcade and a loft building.
V. This limitation enables the mart occupants to ship the orders from another location after the retailer or dealer makes his selection from the samples.

The CORRECT answer is:
A. II, IV, III, I, V
B. IV, III, V, I, II
C. I, III, II, IV, V
D. I, IV, II, III, V

4.____

5.
I. In general, staff-line friction reduces the distinctive contribution of staff personnel.
II. The conflicts, however, introduce an uncontrolled element into the managerial system.
III. On the other hand, the natural resistance of the line to staff innovations probably usefully restrains over-eager efforts to apply untested procedures on a large scale.
IV. Under such conditions, it is difficult to know when valuable ideas are being sacrificed.
V. The relatively weak position of staff, requiring accommodation to the line, tends to restrict their ability to engage in free, experimental innovation.

The CORRECT answer is:
A. IV, II, III, I, V
B. I, V, III, II, IV
C. V, III, I, II, IV
D. II, I, IV, V, III

5.____

KEY (CORRECT ANSWERS)

1. A
2. D
3. D
4. A
5. B

TEST 3

DIRECTIONS: Questions 1 through 4 consist of six sentences which can be arranged in a logical sequence. For each question, select the choice which places the numbered sentences in the MOST logical sequent. *PRINT THE LETTER OF THE CORRECT ANSWER IN THE SPACE AT THE RIGHT.*

1. I. The burden of proof as to each issue is determined before trial and remains upon the same party throughout the trial.
   II. The jury is at liberty to believe one witness' testimony as against a number of contradictory witnesses.
   III. In a civil case, the party bearing the burden of proof is required to prove his contention by a fair preponderance of the evidence.
   IV. However, it must be noted that a fair preponderance of evidence does not necessarily mean a greater number of witnesses.
   V. The burden of proof is the burden which rests upon one of the parties to an action to persuade the trier of the facts, generally the jury, that a proposition he asserts is true.
   VI. If the evidence is equally balanced, or if it leaves the jury in such doubt as to be unable to decide the controversy either way, judgment must be given against the party upon whom the burden of proof rests.
   The CORRECT answer is:
   A. III, II, V, IV, I, VI
   B. I, II, VI, V, III, IV
   C. III, IV, V, I, II, VI
   D. V, I, III, VI, IV, II

   1.____

2. I. If a parent is without assets and is unemployed, he cannot be convicted of the crime of non-support of a child.
   II. The term "sufficient ability" has been held to mean sufficient financial ability.
   III. It does not matter if his unemployment is by choice or unavoidable circumstances.
   IV. If he fails to take any steps at all, he may be liable to prosecution for endangering the welfare of a child.
   V. Under the penal law, a parent is responsible for the support of his minor child only if the parent is "of sufficient ability."
   VI. An indigent parent may meet his obligation by borrowing money or by seeking aid under the provisions of the Social Welfare Law.
   The CORRECT answer is:
   A. VI, I, V, III, II, IV
   B. I, III, V, II, IV, VI
   C. V, II, I, III, VI, IV
   D. I, VI, IV, V, II, III

   2.____

3. I. Consider, for example, the case of a rabble rouser who urges a group of twenty people to go out and break the windows of a nearby factory.
   II. Therefore, the law fills the indicated gap with the crime of inciting to riot.
   III. A person is considered guilty of inciting to riot when he urges ten or more persons to engage in tumultuous and violent conduct of a kind likely to create public alarm.
   IV. However, if he has not obtained the cooperation of at least four people, he cannot be charged with unlawful assembly.

   3.____

93

4.
- V. The charge of inciting to riot was added to the law to cover types of conduct which cannot be classified as either the crime of "riot" or the crime of "unlawful assembly."
- VI. If he acquires the acquiescence of at least four of them, he is guilty of unlawful assembly even if the project does not materialize.

The CORRECT answer is:
- A. III, V, I, VI, IV, II
- B. V, I, IV, VI, II, III
- C. III, IV, I, V, II, VI
- D. V, I, IV, VI, III, II

4.
- I. If, however, the rebuttal evidence presents an issue of credibility, it is for the jury to determine whether the presumption has, in fact, been destroyed.
- II. Once sufficient evidence to the contrary is introduced, the presumption disappears from the trial.
- III. The effect of a presumption is to place the burden upon the adversary to come forward with evidence to rebut the presumption.
- IV. When a presumption is overcome and ceases to exist in the case, the fact or facts which gave rise to the presumption still remain.
- V. Whether a presumption has been overcome is ordinarily a question for the court.
- VI. Such information may furnish a basis for a logical inference.

The CORRECT answer is:
- A. IV, VI, II, V, I, III
- B. III, II, V, I, IV, VI
- C. V, III, VI, IV, II, I
- D. V, IV, I, II, VI, III

KEY (CORRECT ANSWERS)

1. D
2. C
3. A
4. B

PREPARING WRITTEN MATERIAL
EXAMINATION SECTION
TEST 1

DIRECTIONS: The following groups of sentences need to be arranged in an order that makes sense. Select the letter preceding the sequence that represents the BEST sentence order. *PRINT THE LETTER OF THE CORRECT ANSWER IN THE SPACE AT THE RIGHT.*

1. I. A large Naval station on Alameda Island, near Oakland, held many warships in port, and the War Department was worried that if the bridge were to be blown up by the enemy, passage to and from the bay would be hopelessly blocked.
    II. Though many skeptics were opposed to the idea of building such an enormous bridge, the most vocal opposition came from a surprising source: the United States War Department.
    III. The War Department's concerns led to a showdown at San Francisco City Hall between Strauss and the Secretary of War, who demanded to know what would happen if a military enemy blew up the bridge.
    IV. In 1933, by submitting a construction cost estimate of $17 million, an engineer named Joseph Strauss won the contract to build the Golden Gate Bridge of San Francisco, which would then become one of the world's largest bridges.
    V. Strauss quickly ended the debate by explaining that the Golden Gate Bridge was to be a suspension bridge, whose roadway would hang in the air from cables strung between two huge towers, and would immediately sink into three hundred feet of water if it were destroyed.
    The BEST order is:
    A. II, III, I, IV, V   B. I, II, III, V, IV   C. IV, II, I, III, V   D. IV, I, III, V, II

    1.____

2. I. Plastic surgeons have already begun to use virtual reality to map out the complex nerve and tissue structures of a particular patient's face, in order to prepare for delicate surgery.
    II. A virtual reality program responds to these movements by adjusting the images that a person sees on a screen or through goggles, thereby creating an "interactive" world in which a person can see and touch three-dimensional graphic objects.
    III. No more than a computer program that is designed to build and display graphic images, the virtual reality program takes graphic programs a step further by sensing a person's head and body movements.
    IV. The computer technology known as virtual reality, now in its very first stages of development, is already revolutionizing some aspects of contemporary life.
    V. Virtual reality computers are also being used by the space program, most recently to simulate conditions for the astronauts who were launched on a repair mission to the Hubble telescope.

    2.____

The BEST order is:
A. IV, II, I, V, III   B. III, I, V, II, IV   C. IV, III, II, I, V   D. III, I, II, IV, V

3. I. Before you plant anything, the soil in your plant bed should be carefully raked level, a small section at a time, and any clods or rocks that can't be broken up should be removed.
    II. Your plant should be placed in a hole that will position it at the same level it was at the nursery, and a small indentation should be pressed into the soil around the plant in order to hold water near its roots.
    III. Before placing the plant in the soil, lightly separate any roots that may have been matted together in the container, cutting away any thick masses that can't be separated, so that the remaining roots will be able to grow outward.
    IV. After the bed is ready, remove your plant from its container by turning it upside down and tapping or pushing on the bottom —never remove it by pulling on the plant.
    V. When you bring home a small plant in an individual container from the nursery, there are several things to remember while preparing to plant it in your own garden.
    The BEST order is:
    A. V, IV, III, II, I   B. V, II, IV, III, II   C. I, IV, II, III, V   D. I, IV, V, II, III

4. I. The motte and its tower were usually built first, so that sentries could use it as a lookout to warn the castle workers of any danger that might approach the castle.
    II. Though the moat and palisade offered the bailey a good deal of protection, it was linked to the motte by a set of stairs that led to a retractable drawbridge at the motte's gate, to enable people to evacuate onto the motte in case of an attack.
    III. The motte of these early castles was a fortified hill, sometimes as high as one hundred feet, on which stood a palisade and tower.
    IV. The bailey was a clear, level spot below the motte, also enclosed by a palisade, which in turn was surrounded by a large trench or moat.
    V. The earliest castles built in Europe were not the magnificent stone giants that still tower over much of the European landscape, but simpler wooden constructions called motte-and-bailey castles.
    The BEST order is:
    A. V, III, I, IV, II   B. V, IV, I, II, III   C. I, IV, III, II, V   D. I, III, II, IV, V

5. I. If an infant is left alone or abandoned for a short while, its immediate response is to cry loudly, accompanying its screams with aggressive flailing of its legs and limbs.
    II. If a child has been abandoned for a longer period of time, it becomes completely still and quiet, as if realizing that now its only chance for survival is to shut its mouth and remain motionless.
    III. Along with their intense fear of the dark, the crying behavior of human infants offers insights into how prehistoric newborn children might have evolved instincts that would prevent them from becoming victims of predators.

IV. This behavior often surprises people who enter a hospital's maternity ward for the first time and encounter total silence from a roomful of infants.

V. This violent screaming response is quite different from an infant's cries of discomfort or hunger, and seems to serve as either the child's first line of defense against an unwanted intruder, or a desperate attempt to communicate its position to the mother.

The BEST order is:
A. III, II, IV, I, V   B. III, I, V, II, IV   C. I, V, IV, II, III   D. II, IV, I, V, III

6. I. When two cats meet who are strangers, their first actions and gestures determine who the "dominant" cat will be, at least for the time being.

II. Unlike dogs, cats are typically a solitary animal species who avoid social interaction, but they do display specific social responses to each other upon meeting.

III. This is unlikely, however; before such a point of open hostility is reached, one of the cats will usually take the "submissive" position of crouching down while looking away from the other dat.

IV. If a cat desires dominance or sees the other cat as a threat to its territory, it will stare directly at the intruder with a lowered tail.

V. If the other cat responds with a similar gesture, or with the strong defensive posture of an arched back, laid-back ears and raised tail, a fight or chase is likely if neither cat gives in.

The BEST order is:
A. IV, II, I, V, III   B. I, II, IV, V, III   C. I, IV, V, III, II   D. II, I, IV, V, III

7. I. A star or planet's gravitational force can best be explained in this way: anything passing through this "dent" in space will veer toward the star or planet as if it were rolling into a hole.

II. Objects that are massive or heavy, such as stars or planets, "sink" into this surface, creating a sort of dent or concavity in the surrounding space.

III. Black holes, the most massive objects known to exist in space, create dents so large and deep that the space surrounding them actually folds in on itself, preventing anything that falls in —even light —from ever escaping again.

IV. The sort of dent a star or planet makes depends on how massive it is; planets generally have weak gravitational pulls, but stars, which are larger and heavier, make a bigger "dent" that will attract more matter.

V. In outer space, the force of gravity works as if the surrounding space is a soft, flat surface.

The BEST order is:
A. III, V, II, I, IV   B. III, IV, I, V, II   C. V, II, I, IV, III   D. I, V, II, IV, III

8. I. Eventually, the society of Kyoto gave the world one of its first and greatest novels when Japan's most promising writer, Lady Murasaki Shikibu, wrote her chronicle of Kyoto's society, *The Tale of Genji*, which preceded the first European novels by more than 500 years.

II. The society of Kyoto was dedicated to the pleasures of art; the courtiers experimented with new and colorful methods of sculpture, painting, writing, decorative gardening, and even making clothes.

III. Japanese culture began under the powerful authority of Chinese Buddhism, which influenced every aspect of Japanese life from religion to politics and art.
IV. This new, vibrant culture was so sophisticated that all the people in Kyoto's imperial court considered themselves poets, and the line between life and art hardly existed —lovers corresponded entirely through written verses, and even government officials communicated by writing poems to each other.
V. In the eighth century, when the emperor established the town of Kyoto as the capital of the Japanese empire, Japanese society began to develop its own distinctive style.

The BEST order is:
A. V, II, IV, I, III   B. II, I, V, IV, III   C. V, III, IV, I, II   D. III, V, II, IV, I

9. I. Instead of wheels, the HSST uses two sets of magnets, one which sits on the track, and another that is carried by the train; these magnets generate an identical magnetic field which forces the two sets apart.
    II. In the last few decades, railway travel has become less popular throughout the world, because it is much slower than travel by airplane, and not much less expensive.
    III. The HSST's designers say that the train can take passengers from one town to another as quickly as a jet plane —while consuming less than half the energy.
    IV. This repellent effect is strong enough to lift the entire train above the trackway, and the train, literally traveling on air, rockets along at speeds of up to 300 miles per hour.
    V. The revolutionary technology of magnetic levitation, currently being tested by Japan's experimental HSST (High Speed Surface Transport), may yet bring passenger trains back from the dead.

    The BEST order is:
    A. II, V, I, IV, III   B. II, I, IV, III, V   C. V, II, III, I, IV   D. V, I, III, IV, II

10. I. When European countries first began to colonize the African continent, their impression of the African people was of a vast group of loosely organized tribal societies, without any great centralized source of power or wealth.
    II. The legend of Timbuktu persisted until the nineteenth century, when a French adventurer visited Timbuktu and found that raids by neighboring tribesmen had made the city a shadow of its former self.
    III. In the fifteenth century, when the stories of travelers who had traveled Africa's Sudan region began circulating around Europe, this impression began to change.
    IV. In 1470, an Italian merchant named Benedetto Dei traveled to Timbuktu and confirmed these rumors, describing a thriving metropolis where rich and poor people worshipped together in the city's many ornate mosques — there was even a university in Timbuktu, much like its European counterparts, where African scholars pursued their studies in the arts and sciences.

V. The travelers' legends told of an enormous city in the western Sudan, Timbuktu, where the streets were crowded with goods brought by faraway caravans, and where there was a stone palace as large as any in Europe.

The BEST order is:
A. III, V, I, IV, II   B. I, II, IV, III, V   C. I, III, V, IV, II   D. II, I, III, IV, V

11. I. Also, our reference points in sighting the moon make us believe that its size is changing; when the moon is rising through the trees, it seems huge, because our brains unconsciously compare the size of the moon with the size of the trees in the foreground.
II. To most people, the sky itself appears more distant at the horizon than directly overhead, and if the moon's size—which remains constant—is projected from the horizon, the apparent distance of the horizon makes the moon look bigger.
III. Up higher in the sky, the moon is set against tiny stars in the background, which will make the moon seem smaller.
IV. People often wonder why the moon becomes bigger when it approaches the horizon, but most scientists agree that this is a complicated optical illusion, produced by at least three factors.
V. The moon illusion may also be partially explained by a phenomenon that has nothing to do with errors in our perception—light that enters the earth's atmosphere is sometimes refracted, and so the atmosphere may act as a kind of magnifying glass for the moon's image.

The BEST order is:
A. IV, III, V, II, I   B. IV, II, I, III, V   C. V, II, I, III, IV   D. II, I, III, IV, V

11._____

12. I. When the Native Americans were introduced to the horses used by white explorers, they were amazed at their new alternative—here was an animal that was strong and swift, would patiently carry a person or other loads on its back, and they later discovered, was right at home on the plains.
II. Before the arrival of European explorers to North America, the natives of the American plains used large dogs to carry their travois-long lodgepoles loaded with clothing, gear, and food.
III. These horses, it is now known, were not really strangers to North America; the very first horses originated here, on this continent, tens of thousands of years ago, and migrated into Asia across the Bering Land Bridge, a strip of land that used to link our continent with the Eastern world.
IV. At first, the natives knew so little about horses that at least one tribe tried to feed their new animals pieces of dried meat and animal fat, and were surprised when the horses turned their heads away and began to eat the grass of the prairie.
V. The American horse eventually became extinct, but its Asian cousins were reintroduced to the New World when the European explorers brought them to live among the Native Americans.

The BEST order is:
A. II, I, IV, III, V   B. II, IV, I, III, V   C. I, II, IV, III, V   D. I, III, V, II, IV

12._____

13.
   I. The dress worn by the dancer is believed to have been adorned in the past by shells which would strike each other as the dancer performed, creating a lovely sound.
   II. Today's jingle-dress is decorated with the tin lids of snuff cans, which are rolled into cones and sewn onto the dress,
   III. During the jingle-dress dance, the dancer must blend complicated footwork with a series of gentle hos that cause the cones to jingle in rhythm to a drumbeat.
   IV. When contemporary Native American tribes meet for a pow-wow, one of the most popular ceremonies to take place is the women's jingle-dress dance.
   V. Besides being more readily available than shells, the lids are thought by many dancers to create a softer, more subtle sound.
   The BEST order is:
   A. II, IV, V, I, III B. IV, II, I, III, V C. II, I, III, V, IV D. IV, I, II, V, III

14.
   I. If a homeowner lives where seasonal climates are extreme, deciduous shade trees—which will drop their leaves in the winter and allow sunlight to pass through the windows—should be planted near the southern exposure in order to keep the house cool during the summer.
   II. This trajectory is shorter and lower in the sky than at any other time of year during the winter, when a house most requires heating; the northern-facing parts of a house do not receive any direct sunlight at all.
   III. In designing an energy-efficient house, especially in colder climates, it is important to remember that most of the house's windows should face south.
   IV. Though the sun always rises in the east and sets in the west, the sun of the northern hemisphere is permanently situated in the southern portion of the sky.
   V. The explanation for why so many architects and builders want this "southern exposure" is related to the path of the sun in the sky.
   The BEST order is:
   A. III, I, V, IV, II B. III, V, IV, II, I C. I, III, IV, II, V D. I, II, V, IV, III

15.
   I. His journeying lasted twenty-four years and took him over an estimated 75,000 miles, a distance that would not be surpassed by anyone other than Magellan—who sailed around the world—for another six hundred years.
   II. Perhaps the most far-flung of these lesser-known travelers was Ibn Batuta, an African Moslem who left his birthplace of Tangier in the summer of 1325.
   III. Ibn Batuta traveled all over Africa and Asia, from Niger to Peking, and to the islands of Maldive and Indonesia.
   IV. However, a few explorers of the Eastern world logged enough miles and adventures to make Marco Polo's voyage look like an evening stroll.
   V. In America, the most well-known of the Old World's explorers are usually Europeans such as Marco Polo, the Italian who brought many elements of Chinese culture to the Western world.
   The BEST order is:
   A. V, IV, II, III, I B. V, IV, III, II, I C. III, II, I, IV, V D. II, III, I, IV, V

16.
   I. In the rainforests of South America, a rare species of frog practices a reproductive method that is entirely different from this standard process.
   II. She will eventually carry each of the tadpoles up into the canopy and drop each into its own little pool, where it will be easy to locate and safe from most predators.
   III. After fertilization, the female of the species, who lives almost entirely on the forest floor, lays between 2 and 16 eggs among the leaf litter at the base of a tree, and stands watch over these eggs until they hatch.
   IV. Most frogs are pond-dwellers who are able to deposit hundreds of eggs in the water and then leave them alone, knowing that enough eggs have been laid to insure the survival of some of their offspring.
   V. Once the tadpoles emerge, the female backs in among them, and a tadpole will wriggle onto her back to be carried high into the forest canopy, where the female will deposit it in a little pool of water cupped in the leaf of a plant.
   The BEST order is:
   A. I, IV, III, II, V   B. I, III, V, II, IV   C. IV, III, II, V, I   D. IV, I, III, V, II

16.____

17.
   I. Eratosthenes had heard from travelers that at exactly noon on June 21, in the ancient city of Aswan, Egypt, the sun cast no shadow in a well, which meant that the sun must be directly overhead.
   II. He knew the sun always cast a shadow in Alexandria, and so he figured that if he could measure the length of an Alexandria shadow at the time when there was no shadow in Aswan, he could calculate the angle of the sun, and therefore the circumference of the earth.
   III. The evidence for a round earth was not new in 1492; in fact, Eratosthenes, an Alexandrian geographer who lived nearly sixteen centuries before Columbus's voyage (275-195 B.C.), actually developed a method for calculating the circumference of the earth that is still in use today.
   IV. Eratosthenes's method was correct, but his result—28,700 miles—was about 15 percent too high, probably because of the inaccurate ancient methods of keeping time, and because Aswan was not due south of Alexandria, as Eratosthenes had believed.
   V. When Christopher Columbus sailed across the Atlantic Ocean for the first time in 1492, there were still some people in the world who ignored scientific evidence and believed that the earth was flat, rather than round.
   The BEST order is:
   A. I, II, V, III, IV   B. V, III, IV, I, II   C. V, III, I, II, IV   D. III, V, I, II, IV

17.____

18.
   I. The first name for the child is considered a trial naming, often impersonal and neutral, such as the Ngoni name *Chabwera*, meaning "it has arrived."
   II. This sort of name is not due to any parental indifference to the child, but is a kind of silent recognition of Africa's sometimes high infant death rate; most parents ease the pain of losing a child with the belief that it is not really a person until it has been given a final name.
   III. In many tribal African societies, families often give two different names to their children, at different periods in time.
   IV. After the trial naming period has subsided and it is clear that the child will survive, the parents choose a final name for the child, an act that symbolically completes the act of birth.

18.____

V. In fact, some African first-given names are explicitly uncomplimentary, translating as "I am dead" or "I am ugly," in order to avoid the jealousy of ancestral spirits who might wish to take a child that is especially healthy or attractive.

The BEST order is:
   A. III, I, II, V, IV   B. III, IV, II, I, V   C. IV, III, I, II, V   D. IV, V, III, I, II

19.   I. Though uncertain of the definite reasons for this behavior, scientists believe the birds digest the clay in order to counteract toxins contained in the seeds of certain fruits that are eaten by macaws.
   II. For example, all macaws flock to riverbanks at certain times of the year to eat the clay that is found in river mud.
   III. The macaws of South America are not only among the largest and most beautifully colored of the world's flying birds, but they are also one of the smartest.
   IV. It is believed that macaws are forced to resort to these toxic fruits during the dry season, when foods are more scarce.
   V. The macaw's intelligence has led to intense study by scientists, who have discovered some macaw behaviors that have not yet been explained.

The BEST order is:
   A. III, IV, I, II, V   B. III, V, II, I, IV   C. V, II, I, IV, III   D. IV, I, II, III, V

20.   I. Although Maggie Kuhn has since passed away, the Gray Panthers are still waging a campaign to reinstate the historical view of the elderly as people whose experience allows them to make their greatest contribution in their later years.
   II. In 1972, an elderly woman named Maggie Kuhn responded to this sort of treatment by forming a group called the Gray Panthers, an organization of both old and young adults with the common goal of creating change.
   III. This attitude is reflected strongly in the way elderly people are treated by our society; many are forced into early retirement, or are placed in rest homes in which they are isolated from their communities.
   IV. Unlike most other cultures around the world, Americans tend to look upon old age with a sense of dread and sadness.
   V. Kuhn believed that when the elderly are forced to withdraw into lives that lack purpose, society loses one of its greatest resources: people who have a lifetime of experience and wisdom to offer their communities.

The BEST order is:
   A. IV, III, II, V, I   B. IV, II, I, III, V   C. II, IV, III, V, I   D. II, I, IV, III, V

21.   I. The current theory among most anthropologists is that humans evolved from apes who lived in trees near the grasslands of Africa.
   II. Still, some anthropologists insist that such an invention was necessary for the survival of early humans, and point to the Kung Bushmen of central Africa as a society in which the sling is still used in this way.
   III. Two of these inventions—fire, and weapons such as spears and clubs—were obvious defenses against predators, and there is archaeological evidence to support the theory of their use.

IV. Once people had evolved enough to leave the safety of trees and walk upright, they needed the protection of several inventions in order to survive.
V. But another invention, a feather or fiber sling that allowed mothers to carry children while leaving their hands free to gather roots or berries, would certainly have decomposed and left behind no trace of itself.

The BEST order is:
A. I, II, III, V, IV   B. IV, I, II, III, V   C. I, IV, III, V, II   D. IV, III, V, II, I

22. I. The person holding the bird should keep it in hot water up to its neck, and the person cleaning should work a mild solution of dishwashing liquid into the bird's plumage, paying close attention to the head and neck.
II. When rinsing the bird, after all the oil has been removed, the running water should be directed against the lay of its feathers, until water begins to bead off the surface of the feathers—a sign that all the detergent has been rinsed out.
III. If you have rescued a sea bird from an oil spill and want to restore it to clean and normal living, you need a large sink, a constant supply of running hot water (a little over 100°F), and regular dishwashing liquid.
IV. This cleaning with detergent solution should be repeated as many times as it takes to remove all traces of oil from the bird's feathers, sometime over a period of several days.
V. But before you begin to clean the bird, you must find a partner because cleaning an oiled bird is a two-person job.

The BEST order is:
A. III, I, II, IV, V   B. III, V, I, IV, II   C. III, I, IV, V, II   D. III, IV, V, I, II

23. I. The most difficult time of year for the Tsaatang is the spring calving, when the reindeer leave their wintering ground and rush to their accustomed calving place, without stopping by night or by day.
II. Reindeer travel in herds, and though some animals are tamed by the Tsaatang for riding or milking, the herds are allowed to roam free.
III. This journey is hard for the Tsaatang, who carry all their possessions with them, but once it's over it proves worthwhile; the Tsaatang can immediately begin to gather milk from reindeer cows who have given birth.
IV. The Tsaatang, a small tribe who live in the far northwest corner of Mongolia, practice a lifestyle that is completely dependent on the reindeer, their main resource for food, clothing, and transport.
V. The people must follow their yearly migrations, living in portable shelters that resemble Native American tepees.

The BEST order is:
A. I, III, II, V, IV   B. I, IV, II, V, III   C. IV, I, III, V, II   D. IV II, V, I, III

24. I. The Romans later improved this system by installing these heated pipe networks throughout walls and ceilings, supplying heat to even the uppermost floors of a building—a system that, to this day, hasn't been much improved.
II. Air-conditioning, the method by which humans control indoor temperatures, was practiced much earlier than most people think.

III. The earliest heating devices other than open fires were used in 350 B.C. by the ancient Greeks, who directed air that had been heated by underground fires into baked clay pipes that ran under the floor.
IV. Ironically, the first successful cooling system, patented in England in 1831, used fire as its main energy source—fires were lit in the attic of a building, creating an updraft of air that drew cool air into the building through ducts that had underground openings near the river Thames.
V. Cooling buildings was more of a challenge, and wasn't attempted until 1500: a water-based system, designed by Leonardo da Vinci, does not appear to have been successful, since it was never used again.
The BEST order is:
   A. III, V, IV, I, II   B. III, I, II, V, IV   C. II, III, I, V, IV   D. IV, II, III, I, V

25. I. Cold, dry air from Canada passes over the Rocky Mountains and sweeps down onto the plains, where it collides with warm, moist air from the waters of the Gulf of Mexico, and when the two air masses meet, the resulting disturbance sometimes forms a violent funnel cloud that strikes the earth and destroys virtually everything in its path.
II. Hurricanes, storms which are generally not this violent and last much longer, are usually given names by meteorologists, but this tradition cannot be applied to tornados, which have a life span measured in minutes and disappear in the same way as they are born—unnamed.
III. A tornado funnel forms rotating columns of air whose speed reaches three hundred miles an hour—a speed that can only be estimated, because no wind-measuring devices in the direct path of a storm have ever survived.
IV. The natural phenomena known as tornados occur primarily over the Midwestern grasslands of the United States.
V. It is here, meteorologists tell us, that conditions for the formation of tornados are sometimes perfect during the spring months.
The BEST order is:
   A. II IV, V, I, III   B. II, III, I, V, IV   C. IV, V, I, III, II   D. IV, III, I, V, II

KEY (CORRECT ANSWERS)

1.	C	11.	B
2.	C	12.	A
3.	B	13.	D
4.	A	14.	B
5.	B	15.	A
6.	D	16.	D
7.	C	17.	C
8.	D	18.	A
9.	A	19.	B
10.	C	20.	A

21. C
22. B
23. D
24. C
25. C

READING COMPREHENSION
UNDERSTANDING AND INTERPRETING WRITTEN MATERIAL
EXAMINATION SECTION
TEST 1

DIRECTIONS: Each question or incomplete statement is followed by several suggested answers or completions. Select the one that BEST answers the question or completes the statement. *PRINT THE LETTER OF THE CORRECT ANSWER IN THE SPACE AT THE RIGHT.*

Questions 1-4.

DIRECTIONS: Questions 1 through 4 are to be answered SOLELY on the basis of the following passage.

Those engaged in the exercise of First Amendment rights by pickets, marches, parades, and open-air assemblies are not exempted from obeying valid local traffic ordinances. In a recent pronouncement, Mr. Justice Baxter, speaking for the Supreme Court, wrote:

The rights of free speech and assembly, while fundamental to our democratic society, still do not mean that everyone with opinions or beliefs to express may address a group at any public place and at any time. The constitutional guarantee of liberty implies the existence of an organized society maintaining public order, without which liberty itself would be lost in the excesses of anarchy. The control of travel on the streets is a clear example of governmental responsibility to insure this necessary order. A restriction in that relation, designed to promote the public convenience in the interest of all, and not susceptible to abuses of discriminatory application, cannot be disregarded by the attempted exercise of some civil rights which, in other circumstances, would be entitled to protection. One would not be justified in ignoring the familiar red light because this was thought to be a means of social protest. Governmental authorities have the duty and responsibility to keep their streets open and available for movement. A group of demonstrators could not insist upon the right to cordon off a street, or entrance to a public or private building, and allow no one to pass who did not agree to listen to their exhortations.

1. Which of the following statements BEST reflects Mr. Justice Baxter's view of the relationship between liberty and public order?

    A. Public order cannot exist without liberty.
    B. Liberty cannot exist without public order.
    C. The existence of liberty undermines the existence of public order.
    D. The maintenance of public order insures the existence of liberty.

2. According to the above passage, local traffic ordinances result from

    A. governmental limitations on individual liberty
    B. governmental responsibility to insure public order
    C. majority rule as determined by democratic procedures
    D. restrictions on expression of dissent

3. The above passage suggests that government would be acting improperly if a local traffic ordinance

   A. was enforced in a discriminatory manner
   B. resulted in public inconvenience
   C. violated the right of free speech and assembly
   D. was not essential to public order

4. Of the following, the MOST appropriate title for the above passage is

   A. THE RIGHTS OF FREE SPEECH AND ASSEMBLY
   B. ENFORCEMENT OF LOCAL TRAFFIC ORDINANCES
   C. FIRST AMENDMENT RIGHTS AND LOCAL TRAFFIC ORDINANCES
   D. LIBERTY AND ANARCHY

Questions 5-8

DIRECTIONS: Questions 5 through 8 are to be answered SOLELY on the basis of the following passage

On November 8, 1976, the Supreme Court refused to block the payment of Medicaid funds for elective abortions. The Court's action means that a new Federal statute that bars the use of Federal funds for abortions unless abortion is necessary to save the life of the mother will not go into effect for many months, if at all.

A Federal District Court in Brooklyn ruled the following month that the statute was unconstitutional and ordered that Federal reimbursement for the costs of abortions continue on the same basis as reimbursements for the costs of pregnancy and childbirth-related services.

Technically, what the Court did today was to deny a request by Senator Howard Ramsdell and others for a stay blocking enforcement of the District Court order pending appeal. The Court's action was a victory for New York City. The City's Health and Hospitals Corporation initiated one of the two lawsuits challenging the new statute that led to the District Court's decision. The Corporation also opposed the request for a Supreme Court stay of that decision, telling the Court in a memorandum that a stay would subject the Corporation to a *grave and irreparable injury*.

5. According to the above passage, it would be CORRECT to state that the Health and Hospitals Corporation

   A. joined Senator Ramsdell in his request for a stay
   B. opposed the statute which limited reimbursement for the cost of abortions
   C. claimed that it would experience a loss if the District Court order was enforced
   D. appealed the District Court decision

6. The above passage indicates that the Supreme Court acted in DIRECT response to

   A. a lawsuit initiated by the Health and Hospitals Corporation
   B. a ruling by a Federal District Court
   C. a request for a stay
   D. the passage of a new Federal statute

7. According to the above passage, it would be CORRECT to state that the Supreme Court

   A. blocked enforcement of the District Court order
   B. refused a request for a stay to block enforcement of the Federal statute
   C. ruled that the new Federal statute was unconstitutional
   D. permitted payment of Federal funds for abortion to continue

8. Following are three statements concerning abortion that might be correct:
   I. Abortion costs are no longer to be Federally reimbursed on the same basis as those for pregnancy and childbirth
   II. Federal funds have not been available for abortions except to save the life of the mother
   III. Medicaid has paid for elective abortions in the past

   According to the passage above, which of the following CORRECTLY classifies the above statements into those that are true and those that are not true?

   A. I is true, but II and III are not.
   B. I and III are true, but II is not.
   C. I and II are true, but III is not.
   D. III is true, but I and II are not.

Questions 9-12.

DIRECTIONS: Questions 9 through 12 are to be answered SOLELY on the basis of the following passage.

A person may use physical force upon another person when and to the extent he reasonably believes such to be necessary to defend himself or a third person from what he reasonably believes to be the use or imminent use of unlawful physical force by such other person, unless (a) the latter's conduct was provoked by the actor himself with intent to cause physical injury to another person; or (b) the actor was the initial aggressor; or (c) the physical force involved is the product of a combat by agreement not specifically authorized by law.

A person may not use deadly physical force upon another person under the circumstances specified above unless (a) he reasonably believes that such other person is using or is about to use deadly physical force. Even in such case, however, the actor may not use deadly physical force if he knows he can, with complete safety, as to himself and others avoid the necessity of doing so by retreating; except that he is under no duty to retreat if he is in his dwelling and is not the initial aggressor; or (b) he reasonably believes that such other person is committing or attempting to commit a kidnapping, forcible rape, or forcible sodomy.

9. Jones and Smith, who have not met before, get into an argument in a tavern. Smith takes a punch at Jones, but misses. Jones then hits Smith on the chin with his fist. Smith falls to the floor and suffers minor injuries.
   According to the above passage, it would be CORRECT to state that _____ justified in using physical force.

   A. only Smith was
   B. only Jones was
   C. both Smith and Jones were
   D. neither Smith nor Jones was

10. While walking down the street, Brady observes Miller striking Mrs. Adams on the head with his fist in an attempt to steal her purse.
    According to the above passage, it would be CORRECT to state that Brady would

    A. not be justified in using deadly physical force against Miller since Brady can safely retreat
    B. be justified in using physical force against Miller but not deadly physical force
    C. not be justified in using physical force against Miller since Brady himself is not being attacked
    D. be justified in using deadly physical force

11. Winters is attacked from behind by Sharp, who attempts to beat up Winters with a blackjack. Winters disarms Sharp and succeeds in subduing him with a series of blows to the head. Sharp stops fighting and explains that he thought Winters was the person who had robbed his apartment a few minutes before, but now realizes his mistake.
    According to the above passage, it would be CORRECT to state that

    A. Winters was justified in using physical force on Sharp only to the extent necessary to defend himself
    B. Winters was not justified in using physical force on Sharp since Sharp's attack was provoked by what he believed to be Winters' behavior
    C. Sharp was justified in using physical force on Winters since he reasonably believed that Winters had unlawfully robbed him
    D. Winters was justified in using physical force on Sharp only because Sharp was acting mistakenly in attacking him

12. Roberts hears a noise in the cellar of his home, and, upon investigation, discovers an intruder, Welch. Welch moves towards Roberts in a threatening manner, thrusts his hand into a bulging pocket, and withdraws what appears to be a gun. Roberts thereupon strikes Welch over the head with a golf club. He then sees that the *gun* is a toy. Welch later dies of head injuries. According to the above passage, it would be CORRECT to state that Roberts was

    A. justified in using deadly physical force because he reasonably believed Welch was about to use deadly physical force
    B. not justified in using deadly physical force
    C. justified in using deadly physical force only because he did not provoke Welch's conduct
    D. justified in using deadly physical force only because he was not the initial aggressor

Questions 13-16.

DIRECTIONS: Questions 13 through 16 are to be answered SOLELY on the basis of the following passage.

From the beginning, the Supreme Court has supervised the fairness of trials conducted by the Federal government. But the Constitution, as originally drafted, gave the court no such general authority in state cases. The court's power to deal with state cases comes from the Fourteenth Amendment, which became part of the Constitution in 1868. The crucial provision forbids any state to *deprive any person of life, liberty, or property without due process of law.*

The guarantee of *due process* would seem, at the least, to require fair procedure in criminal trials. But curiously the Supreme Court did not speak on the question for many decades. During that time, however, the due process clause was interpreted to bar *unreasonable* state economic regulations, such as minimum wage laws.

In 1915, there came the case of Leo M. Frank, a Georgian convicted of murder in a trial that he contended was dominated by mob hysteria. Historians now agree that there was such hysteria, with overtones of anti-semitism.

The Supreme Court held that it could not look past the findings of the Georgia courts that there had been no mob atmosphere at the trial. Justices Oliver Wendell Holmes and Charles Evans Hughes dissented, arguing that the constitutional guarantee would be *a barren one* if the Federal courts could not make their own inferences from the facts.

In 1923, the case of Moore v. Dempsey involved five Arkansas Blacks convicted of murder and sentenced to death in a community so aroused against them that at one point they were saved from lynching only by Federal troops. Witnesses against them were said to have been beaten into testifying.

The court, though not actually setting aside the convictions, directed a lower Federal court to hold a habeas corpus hearing to find out whether the trial had been fair, or whether the whole proceeding had been *a mask—that counsel, jury, and judge were swept to the fatal end by an irresistible wave of public passion.*

13. According to the above passage, the Supreme Court's INITIAL interpretation of the Fourteenth Amendment

    A. protected state supremacy in economic matters
    B. increased the scope of Federal jurisdiction
    C. required fair procedures in criminal trials
    D. prohibited the enactment of minimum wage laws

14. According to the above passage, the Supreme Court in the Frank case

    A. denied that there had been mob hysteria at the trial
    B. decided that the guilty verdict was supported by the evidence
    C. declined to question the state court's determination of the facts
    D. found that Leo Frank had not received *due process*

15. According to the above passage, the dissenting judges in the Frank case maintained that

    A. due process was an empty promise in the circumstances of that case
    B. the Federal courts could not guarantee certain provisions of the Constitution
    C. the Federal courts should not make their own inferences from the facts in state cases
    D. the Supreme Court had rendered the Constitution *barren*

16. Of the following, the MOST appropriate title for the above passage is 16.____
    A. THE CONDUCT OF FEDERAL TRIALS
    B. THE DEVELOPMENT OF STATES' RIGHTS: 1868-1923
    C. MOORE V. DEMPSEY: A CASE STUDY IN CRIMINAL JUSTICE
    D. DUE PROCESS-THE EVOLUTION OF A CONSTITUTIONAL CORNERSTONE

Questions 17-20.

DIRECTIONS: Questions 17 through 20 are to be answered SOLELY on the basis of the following passage.

The difficulty experienced in determining which party has the burden of proving payment or non-payment is due largely to a lack of consistency between the rules of pleading and the rules of proof. In some cases, a plaintiff is obligated by a rule of pleading to allege non-payment on his complaint, yet is not obligated to prove non-payment on the trial. An action upon a contract for the payment of money will serve as an illustration. In such a case, the plaintiff must allege non-payment in his complaint, but the burden of proving payment on the trial is upon the defendant. An important and frequently cited case on this problem is Conkling v. Weatherwax. In that case, the action was brought to establish and enforce a legacy as a lien upon real property. The defendant alleged in her answer that the legacy had been paid. There was no witness competent to testify for the plaintiff to show that the legacy had not been paid. Therefore, the question of the burden of proof became of primary importance since, if the plaintiff had the burden of proving non-payment, she must fail in her action; whereas if the burden of proof was on the defendant to prove payment, the plaintiff might win. The Court of Appeals held that the burden of proof was on the plaintiff. In the course of his opinion, Judge Vann attempted to harmonize the conflicting cases on this subject, and for that purpose formulated three rules. These rules have been construed and applied to numerous subsequent cases. As so construed and applied, these may be summarized as follows:

Rule 1. In an action upon a contract for the payment of money only, where the complaint does not allege a balance due over and above all payments made, the plaintiff must allege nonpayment in his complaint, but the burden of proving payment is upon the defendant. In such a case, payment is an affirmative defense which the defendant must plead in his answer. If the defendant fails to plead payment, but pleads a general denial instead, he will not be permitted to introduce evidence of payment.

Rule 2. Where the complaint sets forth a balance in excess of all payments, owing to the structure of the pleading, burden is upon the plaintiff to prove his allegation. In this case, the defendant is not required to plead payment as a defense in his answer but may introduce evidence of payment under a general denial.

Rule 3. When the action is not upon contract for the payment of money, but is upon an obligation created by operation of law, or is for the enforcement of a lien where non-payment of the amount secured is part of the cause of action, it is necessary both to allege and prove the fact of nonpayment.

17. In the above passage, the case of Conkling v. Weatherwax was cited PRIMARILY to illustrate   17._____

    A. a case where the burden of proof was on the defendant to prove payment
    B. how the question of the burden of proof can affect the outcome of a case
    C. the effect of a legacy as a lien upon real property
    D. how conflicting cases concerning the burden of proof were harmonized

18. According to the above passage, the pleading of payment is a defense in Rule(s)   18._____

    A. 1, but not Rules 2 and 3
    B. 2, but not Rules 1 and 3
    C. 1 and 3, but not Rule 2
    D. 2 and 3, but not Rule 1

19. The facts in Conkling v. Weatherwax CLOSELY resemble the conditions described in   19._____

    A. Rule #1
    B. Rule #2
    C. Rule #3
    D. none of the rules

20. The MAJOR topic of the above passage may BEST be described as   20._____

    A. determining the ownership of property
    B. providing a legal definition
    C. placing the burden of proof
    D. formulating rules for deciding cases

Questions 21-25.

DIRECTIONS: Questions 21 through 25 are to be answered SOLELY on the basis of the following passage.

The law is quite clear that evidence obtained in violation of Section 605 of the Federal Communications Act is not admissible in Federal court. However, the law as to the admissibility of evidence in state court is far from clear. Had the Supreme Court of the United States made the wiretap exclusionary rule applicable to the states, such confusion would not exist.

In the case of Alton v. Texas, the Supreme Court was called upon to determine whether wiretapping by state and local officers came within the proscription of the Federal statute and, if so, whether Section 605 required the same remedies for its vindication in state courts. In answer to the first question, Mr. Justice Minton, speaking for the court, flatly stated that Section 605 made it a federal crime for anyone to intercept telephone messages and divulge what he learned. The court went on to say that a state officer who testified in state court concerning the existence, contents, substance, purport, effect, or meaning of an intercepted conversation violated the Federal law and committed a criminal act. In regard to the second question, how-ever, the Supreme Court felt constrained by due regard for federal-state relations to answer in the negative. Mr. Justice Minton stated that the court would not presume, in the absence of a clear manifestation of congressional intent, that Congress intended to supersede state rules of evidence.

Because the Supreme Court refused to apply the exclusionary rule to wiretap evidence that was being used in state courts, the states respectively made this decision for themselves. According to hearings held before a congressional committee in 1975, six states authorize wiretapping by statute, 33 states impose total bans on wiretapping, and 11 states have no definite statute on the subject. For examples of extremes, a statute in Pennsylvania will be compared with a statute in New York.

The Pennsylvania statute provides that no communications by telephone or telegraph can be intercepted without permission of both parties. It also specifically prohibits such interception by public officials and provides that evidence obtained cannot be used in court.

The lawmakers in New York, recognizing the need for legal wire-tapping, authorized wiretapping by statute. A New York law authorizes the issuance of an ex parte order upon oath or affirmation for limited wiretapping. The aim of the New York law is to allow court-ordered wiretapping and to encourage the testimony of state officers concerning such wiretapping in court. The New York law was found to be constitutional by the New York State Supreme Court in 1975. Other states, including Oregon, Maryland, Nevada, and Massachusetts, enacted similar laws which authorize court-ordered wiretapping.

To add to this legal disarray, the vast majority of the states, including New Jersey and New York, permit wiretapping evidence to be received in court even though obtained in violation of the state laws and of Section 605 of the Federal act. However, some states, such as Rhode Island, have enacted statutory exclusionary rules which provide that illegally procured wiretap evidence is incompetent in civil as well as criminal actions.

21. According to the above passage, a state officer who testifies in New York State court concerning the contents of a conversation he overheard through a court-ordered wire-tap is in violation of _____ law.

    A. state law but not federal
    B. federal law but not state
    C. federal law and state
    D. neither federal nor state

22. According to the above passage, which of the following statements concerning states statutes on wiretapping is CORRECT?

    A. The number of states that impose total bans on wiretapping is three times as great as the number of states with no definite statute on wiretapping.
    B. The number of states having no definite statute on wiretapping is more than twice the number of states authorizing wiretapping.
    C. The number of states which authorize wiretapping by statute and the number of states having no definite statute on wiretapping exceed the number of states imposing total bans on wiretapping.
    D. More states authorize wiretapping by statute than impose total bans on wiretapping.

23. Following are three statements concerning wiretapping that might be valid:
    I. In Pennsylvania, only public officials may legally intercept telephone communications.
    II. In Rhode Island, evidence obtained through an illegal wiretap is incompetent in criminal, but not civil, actions.
    III. Neither Massachusetts nor Pennsylvania authorizes wiretapping by public officials.

    According to the above passage, which of the following CORRECTLY classifies these statements into those that are valid and those that are not?

    A. I is valid, but II and III are not.
    B. II is valid, but I and III are not.
    C. II and III are valid, but I is not.
    D. None of the statements is valid.

24. According to the above passage, evidence obtained in violation of Section 605 of the Federal Communications Act is inadmissible in

    A. federal court but not in any state courts
    B. federal court and all state courts
    C. all state courts but not in federal court
    D. federal court and some state courts

25. In regard to state rules of evidence, Mr. Justice Minton expressed the Court's opinion that Congress

    A. intended to supersede state rules of evidence, as manifested by Section 605 of the Federal Communications Act
    B. assumed that federal statutes would govern state rules of evidence in all wiretap cases
    C. left unclear whether it intended to supersede state rules of evidence
    D. precluded itself from superseding state rules of evidence through its regard for federal-state relations

KEY (CORRECT ANSWERS)

1. B	11. A
2. B	12. A
3. A	13. D
4. C	14. C
5. B	15. A
6. C	16. D
7. D	17. B
8. D	18. A
9. B	19. C
10. B	20. C

21. B
22. A
23. D
24. D
25. C

TEST 2

DIRECTIONS: Each question or incomplete statement is followed by several suggested answers or completions. Select the one that BEST answers the question or completes the Statement. *PRINT THE LETTER OF THE CORRECT ANSWER IN THE SPACE AT THE RIGHT.*

Questions 1-3.

DIRECTIONS: Questions 1 through 3 are to be answered SOLELY on the basis of the following passage.

The State Assembly has passed a bill that would require all state agencies, public authorities, and local governments to refuse bids in excess of $2,000 from any foreign firm or corporation. The only exceptions to this outright prohibition against public buying of foreign goods or services would be for products not available in this country, goods of a quality unobtainable from an American supplier, and products using foreign materials that are *substantially* manufactured in the United States.

This bill is a flagrant violation of the United States' officially espoused trade principles. It would add to the costs of state and local governments. It could provoke retaliatory action from many foreign governments against the state and other American producers, and foreign governments would be fully entitled to take such retaliatory action under the General Agreement on Tariffs and Trade, which the United States has signed.

The State Senate, which now has the Assembly bill before it, should reject this protectionist legislation out of enlightened regard for the interests of the taxpayers and producers of the State—as well as for those of the nation and its trading partners generally. In this time of unemployment and international monetary disorder, the State—with its reputation for intelligent and progressive law-making—should avoid contributing to what could become a tidal wave of protectionism here and overseas.

1. Under the requirements of the bill passed by the State Assembly, a bid from a foreign manufacturer in excess of $2,000 can be accepted by a state agency or local government only if it meets which one of the following requirements?
The

   A. bid is approved individually by the State Legislature
   B. bidder is willing to accept payment in United States currency
   C. bid is for an item of a quality unobtainable from an American supplier
   D. bid is for an item which would be more expensive if it were purchased from an American supplier

2. The author of the above passage feels that the bill passed by the State Assembly should be

   A. passed by the State Senate and put into effect
   B. passed by the State Senate but vetoed by the Governor
   C. reintroduced into the State Assembly and rejected
   D. rejected by the State Senate

3. The author of the above passage calls the practice of prohibiting purchase of products manufactured by foreign countries

   A. prohibition
   B. protectionism
   C. retaliatory action
   D. isolationism

Questions 4-7.

DIRECTIONS: Questions 4 through 7 are to be answered SOLELY on the basis of the following passage.

Data processing is by no means a new invention. In one form or another, it has been carried on throughout the entire history of civilization. In its most general sense, data processing means organizing data so that it can be used for a specific purpose-a procedure commonly known simply as *record-keeping* or *paperwork*. With the development of modern office equipment, and particularly with the recent introduction of computers, the techniques of data processing have become highly elaborate and sophisticated, but the basic purpose remains the same: Turning raw data into useful information.

The key concept here is usefulness. The data, or input, that is to be processed can be compared to the raw material that is to go into a manufacturing process. The information, or output, that results from data processing—like the finished product of a manufacturer—should be clearly usable. A collection of data has little value unless it is converted into information that serves a specific function.

4. The expression *paperwork*, as it is used in this passage,

   A. shows that the author regards such operations as a waste of time
   B. has the same general meaning as *data processing*
   C. refers to methods of record-keeping that are no longer in use
   D. indicates that the public does not understand the purpose of data processing

5. The above passage indicates that the use of computers has

   A. greatly simplified the clerical work in an office
   B. led to more complicated systems for the handling of data
   C. had no effect whatsoever on data processing
   D. made other modern office machines obsolete

6. Which of the following BEST expresses the basic principle of data processing as it is described in the above passage?

   A. Input-processing-output
   B. Historical record-keeping-modern techniques -specific functions
   C. Office equipment-computer-accurate data
   D. Raw material-manufacturer-retailer

7. According to the above passage, data processing may be described as

   A. a new management technique
   B. computer technology
   C. information output
   D. record-keeping

Questions 8-10.

DIRECTIONS: Questions 8 through 10 are to be answered SOLELY on the basis of the following passage.

A loan receipt is an instrument devised to permit the insurance company to bring an action against the wrongdoer in the name of the insured despite the fact that the insured no longer has any financial interest in the outcome. It provides, in effect, that the amount of the loss is advanced to the insured as a loan which is repayable only up to the extent of any recovery made from the wrongdoer. The insured further agrees to enter and prosecute suit against the wrongdoer in his own name. Such a receipt substitutes a loan for a payment for the purpose of permitting the insurance company to press its action against the wrongdoer in the name of the insured.

8. According to the above passage, the purpose behind the use of a loan receipt is to   8._____

    A. guarantee that the insurance company gets repayment from the person insured
    B. insure repayment of all expenditures to the named insured
    C. make it possible for the insurance company to sue in the name of the policyowner
    D. prevent the wrongdoer from escaping the natural consequences of his act

9. According to the above passage, the amount of the loan which must be paid back to the insurance company equals but does NOT exceed the amount   9._____

    A. of the loss
    B. on the face of the policy
    C. paid to the insured
    D. recovered from the wrongdoer

10. According to the above passage, by giving a loan receipt, the person insured agrees to   10._____

    A. a suit against the wrongdoer in his own name
    B. forego any financial gain from the outcome of the suit
    C. institute an action on behalf of the insurance company
    D. repay the insurance company for the loan received

Questions 11-12.

DIRECTIONS: Questions 11 and 12 are to be answered SOLELY on the basis of the following passage.

Open air markets originally came into existence spontaneously when groups of pushcart peddlers congregated in spots where business was good. Good business induced them to return to these spots daily and, thus, unofficial open air markets arose. These peddlers paid no fees, and the city received no revenue from them. Confusion and disorder reigned in these unsupervised markets; the earliest arrivals secured the best locations, unless or until forcibly ejected by stronger or tougher peddlers. Although the open air markets supplied a definite need in the community, there were many detrimental factors involved in their operation. They were unsightly, created unsanitary conditions in market streets by the deposit of garbage and waste and were a definite obstruction to traffic, as well as a fire hazard.

11. On the basis of the above passage, the MOST accurate of the following statements is:

    A. Each peddler in the original open air markets had his own fixed location.
    B. Open air markets were originally organized by means of agreements between groups of pushcart peddlers.
    C. The locations of these markets depended upon the amount of business the vendors were able to do.
    D. There was confusion and disorder in these open air markets because the peddlers were not required to pay any fees to the city.

12. Of the following, the MOST valid implication which can be made on the basis of the above passage is that the

    A. detrimental aspect of the operations of open air markets was the probable reason for the creation of enclosed markets under the supervision of the Department of Markets
    B. open air markets could not supply any community need without proper supervision
    C. original open air markets were good examples of the operation of fair competition in business
    D. possibility of obtaining a source of revenue was probably the most important reason for the city's ultimate undertaking of the supervision of open air markets

Questions 13-14.

DIRECTIONS: Questions 13 and 14 are to be answered SOLELY on the basis of the following passage.

A person who displays on his window, door, or in his place of business words or letters in Hebraic characters other than the word *kosher,* or any sign, emblem, insignia, six-pointed star, symbol or mark in simulation of same, without displaying in conjunction there-with in English letters of at least the same size as such characters, signs, emblems, insignia or marks, the words *we sell kosher meat and food only* or *we sell non-kosher meat and food only* or *we sell both kosher and non-kosher meat and food,* as the case may be, is guilty of a misdemeanor. Possession of non-kosher meat and food in any place of business advertising the sale of kosher meat and food only is presumptive evidence that the person in possession exposes the same for sale with intent to defraud, in violation of the provisions of this section.

13. Of the following, the MOST valid implication that can be made on the basis of the above passage is that a person who

    A. displays on his window a six-pointed star in addition to the word *kosher* in Hebraic letters is guilty of intent to defraud
    B. displays on his window the word *kosher* in Hebraic characters intends to indicate that he has only kosher food for sale
    C. sells both kosher and non-kosher food in the same place of business is guilty of a misdemeanor
    D. sells only that type of food which can be characterized as neither kosher nor non-kosher, such as fruit and vegetables, without an explanatory sign in English is guilty of intent to defraud

14. Of the following, the one which would constitute a violation of the rules of the above passage is a case in which a person 14._____

    A. displays the word *kosher* on his window in Hebraic letters has only kosher meat and food in the store but has some non-kosher meat in the rear of the establishment
    B. selling both kosher and non-kosher meat and food uses words in Hebraic letters, other than the word *kosher*, on his window and a sign of the same size letters in English stating *we sell both kosher and non-kosher meat and food*
    C. selling only kosher meat and food uses words in Hebraic letters, other than the word *kosher*, on his window and a sign of the same size letters in English stating *we sell kosher meat and food only*
    D. selling only non-kosher meat and food displays a six-pointed star on his window and a sign of the same size letters in English stating *we sell only non-kosher meat and food*

Questions 15-16.

DIRECTIONS: Questions 15 and 16 are to be answered SOLELY on the basis of the following passage.

COMMODITIES IN GLASS BOTTLES OR JARS

The contents of the bottle may be stated in terms of weight or of fluid measure, the weight being indicated in terms of pounds and ounces and the fluid measure being indicated in terms of gallons, quarts, pints, half-pints, gills, or fluid ounces. When contents are liquid, the amount should not be stated in terms of weight. The marking indicating content is to be on a tag attached to the bottle or upon a label. The letters shall be in bold-faced type at least one-ninth of an inch (1/9") in height for bottles or jars having a capacity of a gill, half-pint, pint, or multiples of a pint, and letters at least three-sixteenths of an inch (3/16") in height for bottles of other capacities, on a part of the tag or label free from other printing or ornamentation, leaving a clear space around the marking which indicates the contents.

15. Of the following, the one which does NOT meet the requirements of the above passage is a 15._____

    A. bottle of cooking oil with a label stating *contents—16 fluid ounces* in appropriate sized letters
    B. bottle of vinegar with a label stating *contents—8 ounces avoir.* in appropriate sized letters
    C. glass jar filled with instant coffee with a label stating *contents—1 lb. 3 ozs. avoir.* in appropriate sized letters
    D. glass jar filled with liquid bleach with a label stating *contents—1 quart* in appropriate sized letters

16. Of the following, the one which does meet the requirements of the above passage is a 16._____

    A. bottle filled with a low-calorie liquid sweetener with a label stating *contents—3 fluid ounces* in letters 1/12" high
    B. bottle filled with ammonia solution for cleaning with a label stating *contents—1 pint* in letters 1/10" high

C. jar filled with baking powder with a label stating *contents—$\frac{1}{2}$ pint* in letters $\frac{1}{4}$" high

D. jar filled with hard candy with a label stating *contents—1 lb. avoir.* in letters $\frac{1}{2}$" high

Question 17.

DIRECTIONS: Question 17 is to be answered SOLELY on the basis of the information contained in the following passage.

DEALERS IN SECOND HAND DEVICES

1. It shall be unlawful for any person to engage in or conduct the business of dealing in, trading in, selling, receiving, or repairing condemned, rebuilt, or used weighing or measuring devices without a permit therefor.

2. Such permit shall expire on the twenty-eighth day of February next succeeding the date of issuance thereof.

3. Every person engaged in the above business, within five days after the making of a repair, or the sale and delivery of a repaired, rebuilt, or used weighing or measuring device, shall serve notice in writing on the commissioner giving the name and address of the person for whom the repair has been made or to whom a repaired, rebuilt, or used weighing or measuring device has been sold or delivered, and shall include a statement that such device has been so altered, repaired, or rebuilt as to conform to the regulations of the department.

17. According to the above passage, the MOST accurate of the following statements is: 17.___

A. A permit issued to engage in the business mentioned above, first issued on April 23, 1968, expired on February 28, 1969.
B. A rebuilt or repaired weighing or measuring device should not operate with less error than the tolerances permitted by the regulations of the department.
C. If a used scale in good condition is sold, it is not necessary for the seller to notify the commissioner of the name and address of the buyer.
D. There is a difference in the time required to notify the commissioner of a repair or of a sale of a repaired device.

Questions 18-19.

DIRECTIONS: Questions 18 and 19 are to be answered SOLELY on the basis of the following passage.

A. It shall be unlawful for any person, firm, or corporation to sell or offer for sale at retail for use in internal combustion engines in motor vehicles any gasoline unless such seller shall post and keep continuously posted on the individual pump or other dispensing device from which such gasoline is sold or offered for sale a sign or placard not less than seven inches in height and eight inches in width nor larger than twelve inches in height and twelve inches in width and stating clearly in numbers of uniform size the selling price or prices per gallon of such gasoline so sold or offered for sale from such pump or other dispensing device.

B. The amount of governmental tax to be collected in connection with the sale of such gasoline shall be stated on such sign or placard and separately and apart from such selling price or prices.

18. The one of the following price signs posted on a gasoline pump which would be in violation of the above passage is a sign _____ square inches in size and _____ inches high.

    A. 144; 12   B. 84; 7   C. 72; 12   D. 60; 8

19. According to the above passage, the LEAST accurate of the following statements is:

    A. Gasoline may be sold from a dispensing device other than a pump.
    B. If two different pumps are used to sell the same grade of gasoline, a price sign must appear on each pump.
    C. The amount of governmental tax and the price of the gasoline must not be stated on the same sign.
    D. The sizes of the numbers used on a sign to indicate the price of gasoline must be the same.

Questions 20-21.

DIRECTIONS: Questions 20 and 21 are to be answered SOLELY on the basis of the following passage.

In all systems of weights and measures based on one or more arbitrary fundamental units, the concrete representation of the unit in the form of a standard is necessary, and the construction and preservation of such a standard is a matter of primary importance. Therefore, it is essential that the standard should be so constructed as to be as nearly permanent and invariable as human ingenuity can contrive. The reference of all measures to an original standard is essential for their correctness, and such a standard must be maintained and preserved in its integrity by some responsible authority which is thus able to provide against the use of false weights and measures. Accordingly, from earliest times, standards were constructed and preserved under the direction of kings and priests, and the temples were a favorite place for their deposit. Later, this duty was assumed by the government, and today we find the integrity of standards of weights and measures safeguarded by international agreement.

20. Of the following, the MOST valid implication which can be made on the basis of the above passage is that

    A. fundamental units of systems of weights and measures should be represented by quantities so constructed that they are specific and constant
    B. in the earliest times, standards were so constructed that they were as permanent and invariable as modern ones
    C. international agreement has practically relieved the U.S. government of the necessity of preserving standards of weights and measures
    D. the preservation of standards is of less importance than the ingenuity used in their construction

21. Of the following, the MOST appropriate title for the above passage is 21.____
    A. THE CONSTRUCTION AND PRESERVATION OF STANDARDS OF WEIGHTS AND MEASURES
    B. THE FIXING OF RESPONSIBILITY FOR THE ESTABLISHMENT OF STANDARDS OF WEIGHTS AND MEASURES
    C. THE HISTORY OF SYSTEMS OF WEIGHTS AND MEASURES
    D. THE VALUE OF PROPER STANDARDS IN PROVIDING CORRECT WEIGHTS AND MEASURES

Questions 22-23.

DIRECTIONS: Questions 22 and 23 are to be answered SOLELY on the basis of the following passage.

Accurate weighing and good scales insure that excess is not given just for the sake of good measure. No more striking example of the fundamental importance of correct weighing to the business man is found than in the simple and usual relation where a charge or value is obtained by multiplying a weight by a unit price. For example, a scale may weigh *light,* that is, the actual quantity delivered is in excess by 1 percent. The actual result is that the seller taxes himself. If his profit is supposed to be 10 percent of total sales, an overweight of 1 percent represents 10 percent of that profit. Under these conditions, the situation is as though the seller were required to pay a sales tax equivalent to what he is taxing himself.

22. Of the following, the MOST valid implication which can be made on the basis of the above passage is that 22.____
    A. consistent use of scales that weigh *light* will reduce sellers' profits
    B. no good businessman would give any buyer more than the weight required even if his scale is accurate
    C. the kind of situation described in the above passage could not arise if sales were being made of merchandise sold by the yard
    D. the use of incorrect scales is one of the reasons causing governments to impose sales taxes

23. According to the above passage, the MOST accurate of the following statements is: 23.____
    A. If his scale weighs *light* by an amount of 2 percent, the seller would deliver only 98 pounds when 100 pounds was the amount agreed upon.
    B. If the seller's scale weighs *heavy,* the buyer will receive an amount in excess of what he intended to purchase.
    C. If the seller's scale weighs *light* by an amount of 1 percent, a buyer who agreed to purchase 50 pounds of merchandise would actually receive $50 \frac{1}{2}$ pounds.
    D. The use of a scale which delivers an amount which is in excess of that required is an example of deliberate fraud.

Questions 24-25.

DIRECTIONS: Questions 24 and 25 are to be answered SOLELY on the basis of the following passage.

Food shall be deemed to be misbranded:
1. If its labeling is false or misleading in any particular.

2. If any word, statement, or other information required by or under authority of this article to appear on the label or labeling is not prominently placed thereon with such conspicuousness (as compared with other words, statements, designs, or devices in the labeling) and in such terms as to render it likely to be read and understood by the ordinary individual under customary conditions of purchase and use.

3. If it purports to be or is represented as a food for which a standard of quality has been prescribed and its quality falls below such standard, unless its label bears a statement that it falls below such standard.

24. According to the above passage, the MOST accurate of the following statements is:

    A. A food may be considered misbranded if the label contains a considerable amount of information which is not required.
    B. If a consumer purchased one type of canned food, although he intended to buy another, the food is probably misbranded.
    C. If a food is used in large amounts by a group of people of certain foreign origin, it can be considered misbranded unless the label is in the foreign language with which they are familiar.
    D. The required information on a label is likely to be in larger print than other information which may appear on it.

25. According to the above passage, the one of the following foods which may be considered to be misbranded is a

    A. can of peaches with a label which carries the brand name of the packer but states *Below Standard in Quality*
    B. can of vegetables with a label on which is printed a shield which states *U.S. Grade B*
    C. package of frozen food which has some pertinent information printed on it in very small type which a customer cannot read and which the store manager cannot read when asked to do so by the customer
    D. package of margarine of the same size as the usual package of butter, kept near the butter, but clearly labeled as margarine

KEY (CORRECT ANSWERS)

1. C
2. D
3. B
4. B
5. B

6. A
7. D
8. C
9. D
10. A

11. C
12. A
13. B
14. A
15. B

16. D
17. A
18. C
19. C
20. A

21. D
22. A
23. C
24. D
25. C

PERTINENT EXCERPTS FROM THE SURROGATE'S COURT PROCEDURE ACT (SCPA)

TABLE OF CONTENTS

	Page
ARTICLE 1 – General	1
101-105	1
ARTICLE 2 – Jurisdiction and Powers	4
201-212	4
ARTICLE 3 – Proceedings, Pleadings and Process	7
301-316	7

Surrogate's Court Procedure Act

ARTICLE 1

General

§101. Short title; how cited.
§102. Application of CPLR and other laws.
§103. Definitions.
§104. Application of act; confirmation of previous acts.
§105. Rules for surrogates' courts.

§101. Short title; how cited.-- This act shall be known as the surrogate's court procedure act and may be cited as "SCPA". A provision of this act may be cited by its number without being preceded either by the word "section" or the symbol "j". Reference to an article or section without reference to another law shall be deemed to refer to an article or section of this act

§102. Application of CPLR and other laws.-- The CPLR and other laws applicable to practice and procedure apply in the surrogate's court except where other procedure is provided by this act.

§103. Definitions.--- When used in this act, unless otherwise required by the context, or unless a contrary intent is expressly declared in the provision to be construed, the words, phrases or clauses hereafter shall be construed as follows:

1. Acknowledged. Acknowledged or proved in the same manner as a deed is required to be acknowledged or proved and authenticated to be recorded in that county, except that when executed within the state, no certificate of the county clerk shall be required.

2. Administrator. Any person to whom letters of administration have been issued.

3. Administrator c.t.a. Any person to whom letters of administration with the will annexed have been issued.

4. Administrator d.b.n. Any person to whom letters of administration have been issued as a successor to an administrator.

5. Ancillary administrator. Any person to whom ancillary letters of administration have been issued.

6. Ancillary executor or administrator c.t.a. Any person to whom ancillary letters testamentary or ancillary letters of administration c.t.a. have been issued.

7. Ancillary guardian. Any person to whom ancillary letters of guardianship, whether of the person, property, or both, of an infant have been issued.

8. Beneficiary. Any person entitled to any part or all of the estate of a decedent under a will or in intestacy.

9. Bequest or legacy. A transfer of personal property by will.

10. Court. The surrogate's court, including any judge or surrogate assigned, elected or appointed to serve as judge of the court.

11. Creditor. Any person having a claim against a decedent or his estate.

12. Devise. When used as a noun, a transfer of real property by will. When used as a verb, to transfer real property by will.

13. Devisee. Any person to whom real property is transferred by will.

14. Distributee. Any person entitled to take or share in the property of a decedent under the statutes governing descent and distribution.

15. Domicile. A fixed, permanent and principal home to which a person wherever temporarily located always intends to return.

16. Domiciliary. A person whose domicile is within the state of New York.

17. Donee of a power during minority. Any person granted or deemed to have the power during minority to manage property vested in an infant.

18. Eligible to receive letters. Not disqualified on any of the grounds described in 707.

19. Estate. All of the property of a decedent, infant or trust as originally constituted, and as it from time to time exists during administration.

20. Executor. Any person to whom letters testamentary have been issued.

21. Fiduciary. An administrator, administrator c.t.a., administrator d.b.n., ancillary administrator, ancillary administrator c.t.a., ancillary executor, ancillary guardian, executor, guardian, preliminary executor, temporary administrator, testamentary trustee, to any of whom letters have been issued, and also the donee of a Power during minority and a voluntary administrator and a public administrator acting as administrator or a public administrator or county treasurer to whom letters have been issued.

22. Funeral expense. Includes reasonable expense of a funeral, suitable church or other services as an integral part thereof, expense of interment or other disposition of the body, a burial lot and suitable monumental work thereon and a reasonable expenditure for perpetual care of a burial lot of the decedent.

23. Guardian. Any person to whom letters of guardianship, whether of the person, property or both, of an infant have been issued by a court of this state.

24. Incapacitated person. Any person who for any cause is incapable adequately to protect his rights, although not judicially declared an incompetent.

25. Incompetent. Any person judicially declared incompetent to manage his affairs.

26. Infant. Any person under the age of 18 years; provided, however, that such definition shall not be applicable to any provision relating to the New York Uniform Gifts to Minors Act, nor to 1716.

27. Intestate. A person who dies without leaving a valid will. Where it is used with respect to particular property, a person who dies without effectively disposing of that property by will. When used as an adjective, to property not effectively disposed of by will.

28. Judicial settlement. A proceeding whereby the account of a fiduciary is settled and adjudicated by decree of the court.

29. Legal life tenant. Any person entitled for his life or for the life of another to the possession and use of real or personal property.

30. Legatee. Any person designated to receive a transfer by will of personal property.

31. Letters. Includes letters of administration, letters of administration c.t.a., letters of administration d.b.n., limited letters of administration, ancillary letters of administration, ancillary letters of guardianship, ancillary letters testamentary, letters of guardianship, letters of temporary administration, letters testamentary, preliminary letters testamentary and letters of trusteeship. A testamentary trustee who has qualified without the issuance of letters shall be deemed for the purposes of this act to have received letters of trusteeship.

32. Mailing or mail. A direction to mail or for mailing of process, notice or other paper requires deposit of such process, notice or other paper enclosed in a sealed postpaid envelope, directed to the person to be served or notified, in any post office or other depositary under the exclusive care and custody of the United States Post Office Department.

33. Mailing by registered or certified mail. A direction for mailing of process, notice or other paper by registered or certified mail requires mailing in conformity with the requirements of the United States Post Office Department respecting registered or certified mail, as the case may be.

34. Mailing by registered or certified mail; return receipt requested. Mailing in conformity with the requirements of the United States Post Office Department respecting registered mail with return receipt requested or certified mail with return receipt requested, as the case may be.

35. May. When used in this act, in relation to an act to be performed by the court, means in the discretion of the court.

36. Person interested. Any person entitled either absolutely or contingently to share as beneficiary in the estate. A creditor shall not be deemed a person interested. Where this act provides that a "person interested" may apply for relief, a verified allegation of an interest in fact, suffices for the purpose of the application, although the interest may be disputed, unless or until the fact of interest has been judicially determined and no appeal is pending therefrom.

37. Person under disability. Any person who is (a) an infant, (b) an incompetent, (c) an incapacitated person, (d) unknown or whose whereabouts are unknown or (e) confined as a prisoner who fails to appear under circumstances which the court finds are due to confinement in a penal institution.

38. Preliminary executor. Any person to whom preliminary letters testamentary have been issued.

39. Presumptive distributee. Any person who would be a distributee as defined in this act, if the person alleged to be deceased, absentee or internee were dead.

40. Process. Citation, order to show cause, subpoena and any other mandate of the surrogate's court by which jurisdiction is obtained of a party.

41. Property. Anything that may be the subject of ownership and is real or personal property.

42. Respondent. Every party to a proceeding except a petitioner.

43. Safe deposit company. Any corporation authorized under the banking law to let out receptacles for safe deposit of personal property.

44. Temporary administrator. Any person to whom letters of temporary administration have been issued.

45. Testamentary trustee. Any person to whom letters of trusteeship have been issued.

46. Upon the return of process. The time and place for the return of any process and any adjournment thereof, and implies that due proof has been made that the court has jurisdiction over all parties who appeared, have waived or been duly served.

47. Will. A last will, including all the codicils thereto.

§104. Application of act confirmation of previous acts.-- Each provision of this act relating to the jurisdiction of the surrogate's court to take the proof of a will and to grant letters or regulating the mode of procedure in any manner concerning the estate of the decedent applies unless otherwise expressly declared therein, whether the will was made or the decedent died before or after this act take effect. All acts hitherto of surrogates and officers acting as such by completing and certifying in their own names any uncertified wills, and by signing and certifying in their own names any uncertified records of wills, and of other proofs and examinations taken in the proceedings of probate thereof before their predecessors in office, are hereby confirmed and declared to be valid and in full compliance with the pre-existing statutory requirements.

§105. Rules for surrogates' courts.-- The court in each county may make such rules for the conduct of business in its court as it may deem necessary, not inconsistent with statute and subject to the rules and orders of the administrative board and appellate division applicable thereto.

ARTICLE 2

Jurisdiction and Powers

§201. General jurisdiction of the surrogate's court.
§202. Enumerated proceedings not exclusive.
§203. Jurisdiction of parties and subject matter.
§204. Presumption of jurisdiction.
§205. Effect of exercise of jurisdiction.
§206. Exclusive jurisdiction.
§207. Concurrent jurisdiction of two or more courts over estate of non-domiciliary.
§208. Jurisdiction; how affected by locality of certain assets.
§209. Powers incidental to jurisdiction of the court.
§210. Jurisdictional predicate.
§211. When jurisdiction in personam obtained.
§212. Service of process.

§201. General jurisdiction of the surrogate's court.-- 1. The court has, is granted and shall continue to be vested with all the jurisdiction conferred upon it by the Constitution of the State of New York, and all other authority and jurisdiction now or hereafter conferred upon the court by any general or special statute or provision of law, including this act.

2. This and any grant of jurisdiction to the court shall be deemed an affirmative exercise of the legislative power under 12(e) of article VI of the Constitution and shall in all instances be deemed to include and confer upon the court full equity jurisdiction as to any action, proceeding or other matter over which jurisdiction is or may be conferred.

3. The court shall continue to exercise full and complete general jurisdiction in law and in equity to administer justice in all matters relating to the affairs of decedents, and upon the return of any process to try and determine all questions, legal or equitable, arising between any or all of the parties to any action or proceeding, or between any party and any other person having any claim or interest therein, over whom jurisdiction has been obtained as to any and all matters necessary to be determined in order to make a full, equitable and complete disposition of the matter by such order or decree as Justice requires.

§202. Enumerated proceedings not exclusive.-- The proceedings enumerated in this act shall not be deemed exclusive and the court is empowered in any proceeding, whether or not specifically provided for, to exercise any of the jurisdiction granted to it by this act or other provisions of law, notwithstanding that the jurisdiction sought to be exercised in the proceedmg is or may be exercised in or incidental to a different proceeding.

§203. Jurisdiction of parties and subject matter.-- The court obtains jurisdiction in every case to make a decree or other determination by the existence of the Jurisdictional facts prescribed by statute.

The jurisdiction of the court is exercised by the commencement of a proceeding in the court. All proceedings are special proceedings and are commenced by filing a petition. Personal jurisdiction of parties is obtained by service of process upon the parties or by submission to the jurisdiction of the court by waiver of issuance and service of process, appearance of an adult competent party in person or by attorney or by pleading.

§204. Presumption of jurisdiction.-- Where the jurisdiction of the court to make a decree or other determination is drawn in question collaterally, the jurisdiction is presumptively and in the absence of fraud or collusion, conclusively established by an allegation of the jurisdictional facts contained in a verified pleading. Jurisdiction of the parties is presumptively proved by a recital to that effect in the decree.

§205. Effect of exercise of jurisdiction.-- Jurisdiction once duly exercised over any estate or matter by the court excludes the subsequent exercise of jurisdiction by another surrogate's court over the same estate or matter, except as specially prescribed by law. All further proceedings in the same estate or matter in a surrogate's court must be taken in the same court.

§206. Exclusive jurisdiction.-- The surrogate's court of each county has jurisdiction exclusive of every other surrogate's court over the estate of
    1. any domiciliary of the county at the time of his death, disappearance or internment;
    2. any non-domiciliary of the state who
        (a) left property within that county and no other, or
        (b) left personal property which since his death, disappearance or internment has come into that county and no other and remains unadministered or
        (c) left a cause of action against a domiciliary of that county for damages for the wrongful death of the decedent and who left no property in any other county.

§207. Concurrent jurisdiction of two or more courts over estate of non-domiciliary.-- When an estate or matter may be within the jurisdiction of the surrogates' courts of two or more counties, by virtue of personal or real property of a non-domiciliary decedent being within two or more counties, the court which first exercises jurisdiction thereof by the commencement of the proceeding shall retain jurisdiction thereafter.

§208. Jurisdiction; how affected by locality of certain assets.-- For the purpose of conferring jurisdiction upon the court:
    1. A debt or a cause of action for wrongful death, in favor of a non-domiciliary against a domiciliary, is deemed personal property in the county where the domiciliary, or either of two or more such domiciliaries resides, or if other than a natural person, such domiciliary has its principal office, except that a debt evidenced by a negotiable instrument is deemed for jurisdictional purposes personal property in the county of the situs of the instrument.
    2. An insurance policy upon the life of a nondomiciliary decedent shall have the situs of the principal office in this state of the company or corporation issuing the policy of insurance.
    3. A share of stock of a corporation of this state owned by a non-domiciliary is deemed personal property in the county where the corporation has its principal office.
    4. A life insurance policy or share of stock owned by a non-domiciliary is deemed personal property in the county where the policy or share of stock is situated, the provisions of subdivisions 2 and 3 notwithstanding.

§209. Powers incidental to jurisdiction of the court.-- The court has power:
    1. To open, vacate, modify or set aside any decree or order of the court directing distribution of the property of an estate which was made prior to the probate of and without knowledge of a will which affects such distribution and in the same or a different proceeding, and on notice to the persons or the fiduciaries of the persons to whom the property has been distributed, to make such further and different direction as to such distribution as justice may require, and as an incident thereto, order the refund of any property theretofore distributed erroneously.

2. To sign any decision, decree or order, including orders in transfer and estate tax proceedings, with its usual signature or initials, and all decisions, decrees or orders heretofore or hereafter so signed shall be valid and binding.

3. To transfer for trial in the surrogate's court having jurisdiction any action or proceeding pending in any court other than the supreme court, which affects or relates to the administration of a decedent's estate and to receive for trial any such action or proceeding pending in the supreme court which may by order of the latter court be transferred to the surrogate's court on the prior order of that court.

4. To determine a decedent's interest in any property claimed to constitute a part of his gross estate subject to estate tax, or to be property available for distribution under his will or in intestacy or for payment of claims, end o determine the rights of any persons claiming an interest therein, as against the decedent, or as between themselves, and to construe any instruments made by him affecting such property. Nothing herein provided shall be construed to confer jurisdiction on the court over inter vivos trusts.

5. To settle the account of a fiduciary of a common trust fund as provided in the banking law.

6. To entertain a proceeding under EPTL 81.1.

7. To dismiss any proceeding which the petitioner has neglected to prosecute diligently.

8. To determine any unfinished business pending before its predecessor in office and to sign or certify papers or records left uncompleted or unsigned by its predecessor.

9. In the exercise of its jurisdiction, the court shall have all of the powers that the supreme court would have in like actions and proceedings including, but not limited to, such incidental powers as are necessary to carry into effect all powers expressly conferred herein.

10. The enumeration of powers herein shall not be deemed exclusive.

§210. Jurisdictional predicate.-- 1. Traditional bases. The court shall exercise jurisdiction over persons and property as heretofore or hereafter permitted by law.

2. Additional bases.

(a) The court may exercise personal jurisdiction over any nondomiciliary, or his fiduciary as to any matter within the subject matter jurisdiction of the court arising from any act or omission of the nondomiciiary within the state either in person or through an agent.

(b) The receipt and acceptance of any property paid or distributed out of and as part of the administration of an estate subject to the jurisdiction of the court shall constitute a submission by such recipient to the jurisdiction of the court as to any matter concerning the payment or distribution, including proceedings for the recovery thereof.

§211. When jurisdiction in personam obtained.-- The court may exercise personal jurisdiction over any person as to any matter within the subject matter jurisdiction of the court, if, on analogous facts in an action in the supreme court, such person would be subject to the personal jurisdiction of that court.

§212. Service of Process.-- All processes of the court may be served and executed in any Part of the state and without the state when authorized by law.

ARTICLE 3

Proceedings, Pleadings and Process

§301. Statute of limitations.
§302. Pleadings.
§303. Verification.
§304. Contents of petition.
§305. Process, where returnable.
§306. Contents of citation.
§307. Service of process.
§308. Return day of citation.
§309. When service of process complete.
§310. Who may serve process.
§311. Designee for person under disability.
§312. Additional parties; supplemental process.
§313. Manner of giving notice when not otherwise prescribed.
§314. Proof of service of subpoena or process.
§315. Joinder and representation of persons with future interests.
§316. Process to attorney general where persons unknown.

§301. Statute of limitations.--For the purpose of computing the period of limitation under article 2 of the CPLR, a proceeding is commenced upon the filing of a petition, provided process is issued and service made upon any respondent within 60 days after the date of the filing of the petition, except that when process is served by publication, the first publication be made within 60 days of the filing of the petition.

§302. Pleadings.--1. Unless otherwise provided in this act
   (a) Pleadings shall consist of the petition, answer or objections and account.
   (b) There shall be no other pleading unless directed by the court.
   (c) An answer or objection shall be served upon the return of process or at such later date as directed by the court.
2. Statements in a pleading shall be sufficiently particular to give the court and parties notice of the claim, objection or defense and shall contain a demand for the relief sought.
3. Copies of all pleadings, except an account, shall be served upon any party who has appeared in the proceeding and demanded a copy of all papers be served upon him, and upon all parties upon whom the court by order or oral direction entered in the minutes directs that service be made. A party who fails to comply with this requirement may be treated as a party in default.

§303. Verification.-- All pleadings shall be verified in the manner provided by CPLR 3020.

§304. Contents of petition.-- In addition to such other requirements as may be applicable to the petition in a particular proceeding, a petition must substantially set forth:

1. The title of the proceeding, the name and domicile of the person to whose estate or person the proceeding relates and of the petitioner.

2. The facts upon which the jurisdiction of the court depends in the particular proceeding.

3. So far as they can be ascertained with due diligence, the names and addresses of all the persons interested upon whom service of process is required or concerning whom the court is required to have information; and in addition there shall be shown by petition or affidavit in form satisfactory to the court, the following:

(a) If any person be an infant, his age, the date of his birth, whether he has a guardian, whether his father, or if he be dead, his mother, is living, his connection with the estate, and the names and addresses of such persons and the person with whom the infant resides.

(b) If any person be an incompetent, the name and address of his committee, if any, and of the person or institution having his care and custody and if there be no committee, the name and address of an adult relative or friend having an interest in his welfare.

(c) If any person be an incapacitated person, the facts regarding his incapacity and if confined, the name and address of the institution having his care and custody and the name and address of an adult relative or friend having an interest in his welfare.

(d) if any person be unknown or his name or whereabouts be unknown, a general description of such person, showing his connection with the estate and his interest in the proceeding and the facts showing what effort has been made to ascertain his name or whereabouts.

(e) If any person be a prisoner confined in this state or elsewhere, the name and address of the institution in which he is confined, and the name and address of an adult relative or friend having an interest in his welfare.

(f) If any person be included in a class, and his name be unknown, the names and addresses

of those persons of the class who are known and a general description of all other persons belonging to the class, their connection with the estate, and their interest in the proceeding.

4. That there are no other persons than those mentioned interested in the application or proceeding.

5. A request for the relief sought.

§305. Process, where returnable.-- The process of a surrogate's court, except where otherwise prescribed by law, must be trade returnable before the court from which it was issued.

§306. Citation.--1. A citation must be substantially set forth:
- (a) The name and domicile of the person to whose estate or person the proceeding relates and of the petitioner.
- (b) The names of all persons to be served who have not waived issuance and service of process, or have not appeared. Where the number of persons of any class to be served exceeds 50, it need not specify the name of any person of the class but may be directed to the class by such appropriate designation as the court deems adequate.
- (c) The time when and the place where the citation is returnable, which time must be not more than 4 months after the date of issuance.
- (d) The object of the proceeding and the relief sought.
- (e) The date when issued.
- (f) The name, address and telephone number of the petitioner's attorney.

2. In addition it must substantially set forth:

(a) Where the names of some persons to be served comprising a class are unknown, the names of those persons of the class who are known and a general description of all other persons belonging to the class, showing their interest in the proceeding.

(b) Where the persons to be served are unknown, a general description of such persons, showing their interest in the proceeding.

In either of such cases, where the petitioner is ignorant of the name of a person in the citation by a fictitious name or so much of his name and identity as is known.

3. The citation shall be in substantially such form as may be provided by the Official Forms appended to this act.

4. The citation shall be attested in the name of the judge of the court and by the seal of the court, the original shall be filed by the clerk and a copy thereof shall be furnished to the peititioner.

§307. Service of process.--1. Service by personal delivery. Service of the process may be made on any person by personal delivery to him of a copy of the process either within or without the state.

2. Service by court order. As an alternative to service under subdivision 1, service may be made in the manner directed by the court: but such service, except as provided by subdivision 5, shall not be ordered upon a domiciliary natural person unless it be shown that with due diligence, service by personal delivery within the state cannot be effected. Any proof necessary hereunder may be submitted in the petition or by affidavit. The court may direct service by any one or more of the following methods, which shall not, however, be exclusive:

(a) service by publication, such as is provided by CPLR 316, subject to 308 and 309, and to such variations of CPLR 316 as the court may provide, except that

(i) where the aggregate value of the interest in the estate of nil persons to be served by publication amounts to less than $10,000 publication in only 1 newspaper shall be required, or

(ii) where a person is alleged to be within a country with which the United States of America is at war or a place with which the United States of America does not maintain postal communication, the court may direct that a copy of the process shall be mailed on behalf of such person to the officer who may have been appointed to take possession of the property of alien enemies, or

(iii) where the person to be served is an absentee or alleged to be deceased, the court may direct that in addition to the foregoing requirements, the process be published in a newspaper published at or near the place where the absentee was last known to be.

(iv) in an adoption proceeding under article seven of the domestic relations law or in a proceeding under section three hundred eightyfour-b of the social services law, a single publication in only one newspaper shall be sufficient.

(b) mailing, including air mailing;

(c) registered or certified mail with or without return receipt requested;

(d) substituted service such as is provided by CPLR 308 (2) and (4), within or without the state, subject to 308 and 309, and to such variations of CPLR 308 as the court may provide;

(e) service within or without the state, by personal delivery to a person duly designated by respondent to receive process in his behalf, or to a person whose relationship, whatever its character, and by blood or otherwise to the respondent, indicates in the circumstances the probability that actual notice will reach the latter through him;

(f) if the interest of a non-domiciliary alien in the estate is less than $500 or his address is unknown or such estate's gross assets are less than $5,000, by delivery of a copy of the process to a consular official of the alien's nation.

3. Service upon an infant. Service upon an infant requires that service of process he made upon any one of the following: his ather, his mother, his guardian, any adult person having the care and control of him or with whom he resides, or such person interested in his welfare or education as the court shall by order direct, where it appears to the satisfaction of the court that need for such order exists; and if the infant be of the age of 14 years or over, also upon the infant in person.

4. Service upon an incompetent or persons other than natural persons. Unless this act otherwise provides or the court in a given proceeding otherwise directs, CPLR 307, 309(b), 310, 311, 312 and 1025 are applicable to service under the foregoing subdivisions of this section.

5. Service where more than 25 creditors. When more than 25 creditors are parties process may be served on them by mailing a copy f the process to each of them whether or not they be natural domiciliaries.

§308. Return day of citation.--1. Based on place of service. Except as otherwise provided in subdivisions 2 and 3, the time of the return of a citation shall be governed by the following paragraphs:

(a) The citation shall be served at least the following number of days before the return day:

(i) 10 days if the person is served within the state;

(ii) 20 days if the person is served without the state but within the United States, the District of Columbia, the Commonwealth of Puerto Rico or the possessions or territories of the United States; and

(iii) 30 days in all other cases.

(b) The time periods set forth under paragraph (a) of this subdivision shall commence to run from the time that service is complete as provided in 309.

2. Service by publication. If served by publication, the return day shall not be earlier than the day service is completed, as provided in 309.

3. Service on consular official. If served upon a consular official pursuant to 307, subdivision 2(f), it shall be served at least 30 days prior the return day.

4. For the purpose of fixing the time with which a process must be served, service upon clerk of the court, pursuant to designation is personal service upon the fiduciary within the where the letters of the fiduciary were issued.

§309. When service of process complete.--1. Service by personal delivery. The service of process is complete immediately upon personal delivery to the respondent when service is so made.

2. Service by other means. Unless the court directs otherwise, the service of process shall be complete when served by:

(a) mailing or by registered or certified mail, with or without return receipt requested, upon the mailing thereof;

(b) substituted service, upon the delivery or affixing and the mailing thereof, whichever is dune last;

(c) personal delivery to a person duly designated by the respondent, or to a person or consular official designated by the court by order to be served in respondent's behalf, upon such personal delivery;

(d) publication, on the 28th day after the first publication; or

(e) any other means, as the court directs.

§310. Who may serve process.--1. Any person over the age of 18 years, although a party, may serve process of the court within the state.

2. Personal service of process without the state may be made in the same manner as within the state by any of the persons authorized by CPLR 313 even though a party to the proceeding.

§311. Designee for person under disability.-- Whenever the person to be served is a person under disability, whether or not a party so requests, the court may in the interest of such person, require by order or direction in the minutes that a copy of the process issued be delivered to a person designated, in the manner and within the time specified. The person so designated shall have with respect to the proceeding while so designated, in behalf of such person, until the return of process and such further time as directed by the court, the same powers and duties as a guardian ad litem and is authorized to admit service of such process.

§312. Additional parties; supplemental process.-- The court may issue a supplemental process at any time and require any party to procure it and cause it to be served in conformity with the provisions of 307 and 308 on any person in any proceeding, so that any person necessary or proper to a final determination therein may be made a party thereto.

§313. Manner of giving notice when not otherwise prescribed.-- Whenever the manner of giving notice is not otherwise prescribed, the court may direct both as to the form of notice and the manner and time of service thereof. Such direction may be indicated on the process or endorsed upon the application with the same force and effect as if incorporated in an order.

§314. Proof of service of subpoena or process.-- Proof of service of a subpoena or process shall be made in the manner and form prescribed by CPLR 306 and 4532, provided, however, that a writing admitting service shall not be sufficient if made by an infant under the age of 16 years or an incompetent. Any person of the age of 16 years or over required to be served may in writing admit service of process.

§315. Joinder and representation of persons with future interests.-- 1. The provisions of this section shall apply in any proceeding in which all persons interested in the estate are required to be served with process and in which the persons interested include persons entitled to future interests in the estate to which the proceeding relates.

2. Representation in remainders to a class,
  (a) Where an interest in the estate has been limited as follows, it shall not be necessary to serve process on any other person than as herein provided:
  (i) In any contingency to the persons who shall compose a certain class upon the happening of a future event, the persons in being who would constitute the class if such event had happened immediately before the commencement of the proceeding.
  (ii) To a person who is a party to the proceeding and the same interest has been further limited upon the happening of a future event to a class of persons described in terms of their relationship to such party, the party to the proceeding.

(iii) To unborn or unascertained persons, none of such persons, but if it appears that there is no certain or presumptive remainderman in being or ascertained, the court shall appoint a guardian ad litem to represent or protect the persons who eventually may become entitled to the interest.

(b) Where a party to the proceeding has a power of appointment it shall not be necessary to serve the potential appointees.

3. Representation of contingent remaindermen.

Where an interest in the estate has been limited to a person who is a party to the proceeding and the same interest has been further limited upon the happening of a future event to any other person it shall not be necessary to serve such other person.

4. Representation in probate proceeding. In a proceeding for probate of a will the interests of the respective persons specified in subdivisions 2(a)(ii) and 3 of this section shall be deemed to be the same interest, whether or not their respective interests are in income or in principal or in both, provided that they are beneficiaries of the same trust or fund, that they have a common interest in proving the will and that the person who is a party under subdivision 2(a)(ii) or the person to whom the interest has been limited under subdivision 3 would not receive greater financial benefit if the will were denied probate.

5. The decree or order entered in any such proceeding shall be binding and conclusive on any person upon whom service of process is not required.

6. Notwithstanding the foregoing, if the court deems that the representation of a person's interest is or may be inadequate it may require that he be served.

§316. Process to attorney general where persons unknown.-- In every case where it appears that there is no distributee or that it is not known whether or not there be such, the process shall be issued to the attorney general of the state.

GLOSSARY OF LEGAL TERMS

TABLE OF CONTENTS

	Page
Action ... Affiant	1
Affidavit ... At Bar	2
At Issue ... Burden of Proof	3
Business ... Commute	4
Complainant ... Conviction	5
Cooperative ... Demur (v.)	6
Demurrage ... Endorsement	7
Enjoin ... Facsimile	8
Factor ... Guilty	9
Habeas Corpus ... Incumbrance	10
Indemnify ... Laches	11
Landlord and Tenant ... Malice	12
Mandamus ... Obiter Dictum	13
Object (v.) ... Perjury	14
Perpetuity ... Proclamation	15
Proffered Evidence ... Referee	16
Referendum ... Stare Decisis	17
State ... Term	18
Testamentary ... Warrant (Warranty) (v.)	19
Warrant (n.) ... Zoning	20

GLOSSARY OF LEGAL TERMS

A

ACTION - "Action" includes a civil action and a criminal action.
A FORTIORI - A term meaning you can reason one thing from the existence of certain facts.
A POSTERIORI - From what goes after; from effect to cause.
A PRIORI - From what goes before; from cause to effect.
AB INITIO - From the beginning.
ABATE - To diminish or put an end to.
ABET - To encourage the commission of a crime.
ABEYANCE - Suspension, temporary suppression.
ABIDE - To accept the consequences of.
ABJURE - To renounce; give up.
ABRIDGE - To reduce; contract; diminish.
ABROGATE - To annul, repeal, or destroy.
ABSCOND - To hide or absent oneself to avoid legal action.
ABSTRACT - A summary.
ABUT - To border on, to touch.
ACCESS - Approach; in real property law it means the right of the owner of property to the use of the highway or road next to his land, without obstruction by intervening property owners.
ACCESSORY - In criminal law, it means the person who contributes or aids in the commission of a crime.
ACCOMMODATED PARTY - One to whom credit is extended on the strength of another person signing a commercial paper.
ACCOMMODATION PAPER - A commercial paper to which the accommodating party has put his name.
ACCOMPLICE - In criminal law, it means a person who together with the principal offender commits a crime.
ACCORD - An agreement to accept something different or less than that to which one is entitled, which extinguishes the entire obligation.
ACCOUNT - A statement of mutual demands in the nature of debt and credit between parties.
ACCRETION - The act of adding to a thing; in real property law, it means gradual accumulation of land by natural causes.
ACCRUE - To grow to; to be added to.
ACKNOWLEDGMENT - The act of going before an official authorized to take acknowledgments, and acknowledging an act as one's own.
ACQUIESCENCE - A silent appearance of consent.
ACQUIT - To legally determine the innocence of one charged with a crime.
AD INFINITUM - Indefinitely.
AD LITEM - For the suit.
AD VALOREM - According to value.
ADJECTIVE LAW - Rules of procedure.
ADJUDICATION - The judgment given in a case.
ADMIRALTY - Court having jurisdiction over maritime cases.
ADULT - Sixteen years old or over (in criminal law).
ADVANCE - In commercial law, it means to pay money or render other value before it is due.
ADVERSE - Opposed; contrary.
ADVOCATE - (v.) To speak in favor of;
(n.) One who assists, defends, or pleads for another.
AFFIANT - A person who makes and signs an affidavit.

AFFIDAVIT - A written and sworn to declaration of facts, voluntarily made.
AFFINITY- The relationship between persons through marriage with the kindred of each other; distinguished from consanguinity, which is the relationship by blood.
AFFIRM - To ratify; also when an appellate court affirms a judgment, decree, or order, it means that it is valid and right and must stand as rendered in the lower court.
AFOREMENTIONED; AFORESAID - Before or already said.
AGENT - One who represents and acts for another.
AID AND COMFORT - To help; encourage.
ALIAS - A name not one's true name.
ALIBI - A claim of not being present at a certain place at a certain time.
ALLEGE - To assert.
ALLOTMENT - A share or portion.
AMBIGUITY - Uncertainty; capable of being understood in more than one way.
AMENDMENT - Any language made or proposed as a change in some principal writing.
AMICUS CURIAE - A friend of the court; one who has an interest in a case, although not a party in the case, who volunteers advice upon matters of law to the judge. For example, a brief amicus curiae.
AMORTIZATION - To provide for a gradual extinction of (a future obligation) in advance of maturity, especially, by periodical contributions to a sinking fund which will be adequate to discharge a debt or make a replacement when it becomes necessary.
ANCILLARY - Aiding, auxiliary.
ANNOTATION - A note added by way of comment or explanation.
ANSWER - A written statement made by a defendant setting forth the grounds of his defense.
ANTE - Before.
ANTE MORTEM - Before death.
APPEAL - The removal of a case from a lower court to one of superior jurisdiction for the purpose of obtaining a review.
APPEARANCE - Coming into court as a party to a suit.
APPELLANT - The party who takes an appeal from one court or jurisdiction to another (appellate) court for review.
APPELLEE - The party against whom an appeal is taken.
APPROPRIATE - To make a thing one's own.
APPROPRIATION - Prescribing the destination of a thing; the act of the legislature designating a particular fund, to be applied to some object of government expenditure.
APPURTENANT - Belonging to; accessory or incident to.
ARBITER - One who decides a dispute; a referee.
ARBITRARY - Unreasoned; not governed by any fixed rules or standard.
ARGUENDO - By way of argument.
ARRAIGN - To call the prisoner before the court to answer to a charge.
ASSENT - A declaration of willingness to do something in compliance with a request.
ASSERT - Declare.
ASSESS - To fix the rate or amount.
ASSIGN - To transfer; to appoint; to select for a particular purpose.
ASSIGNEE - One who receives an assignment.
ASSIGNOR - One who makes an assignment.
AT BAR - Before the court.

AT ISSUE - When parties in an action come to a point where one asserts something and the other denies it.
ATTACH - Seize property by court order and sometimes arrest a person.
ATTEST - To witness a will, etc.; act of attestation.
AVERMENT - A positive statement of facts.

B

BAIL - To obtain the release of a person from legal custody by giving security and promising that he shall appear in court; to deliver (goods, etc.) in trust to a person for a special purpose.
BAILEE - One to whom personal property is delivered under a contract of bailment.
BAILMENT - Delivery of personal property to another to be held for a certain purpose and to be returned when the purpose is accomplished.
BAILOR - The party who delivers goods to another, under a contract of bailment.
BANC (OR BANK) - Bench; the place where a court sits permanently or regularly; also the assembly of all the judges of a court.
BANKRUPT - An insolvent person, technically, one declared to be bankrupt after a bankruptcy proceeding.
BAR - The legal profession.
BARRATRY - Exciting groundless judicial proceedings.
BARTER - A contract by which parties exchange goods for other goods.
BATTERY - Illegal interfering with another's person.
BEARER - In commercial law, it means the person in possession of a commercial paper which is payable to the bearer.
BENCH - The court itself or the judge.
BENEFICIARY - A person benefiting under a will, trust, or agreement.
BEST EVIDENCE RULE, THE - Except as otherwise provided by statute, no evidence other than the writing itself is admissible to prove the content of a writing. This section shall be known and may be cited as the best evidence rule.
BEQUEST - A gift of personal property under a will.
BILL - A formal written statement of complaint to a court of justice; also, a draft of an act of the legislature before it becomes a law; also, accounts for goods sold, services rendered, or work done.
BONA FIDE - In or with good faith; honestly.
BOND - An instrument by which the maker promises to pay a sum of money to another, usually providing that upon performances of a certain condition the obligation shall be void.
BOYCOTT - A plan to prevent the carrying on of a business by wrongful means.
BREACH - The breaking or violating of a law, or the failure to carry out a duty.
BRIEF - A written document, prepared by a lawyer to serve as the basis of an argument upon a case in court, usually an appellate court.
BURDEN OF PRODUCING EVIDENCE - The obligation of a party to introduce evidence sufficient to avoid a ruling against him on the issue.
BURDEN OF PROOF - The obligation of a party to establish by evidence a requisite degree of belief concerning a fact in the mind of the trier of fact or the court. The burden of proof may require a party to raise a reasonable doubt concerning the existence of nonexistence of a fact or that he establish the existence or nonexistence of a fact by a preponderance of the evidence, by clear and convincing proof, or by proof beyond a reasonable doubt.

    Except as otherwise provided by law, the burden of proof requires proof by a preponderance of the evidence.

BUSINESS, A - Shall include every kind of business, profession, occupation, calling or operation of institutions, whether carried on for profit or not.

BY-LAWS - Regulations, ordinances, or rules enacted by a corporation, association, etc., for its own government.

C

CANON - A doctrine; also, a law or rule, of a church or association in particular.

CAPIAS - An order to arrest.

CAPTION - In a pleading, deposition or other paper connected with a case in court, it is the heading or introductory clause which shows the names of the parties, name of the court, number of the case on the docket or calendar, etc.

CARRIER - A person or corporation undertaking to transport persons or property.

CASE - A general term for an action, cause, suit, or controversy before a judicial body.

CAUSE - A suit, litigation or action before a court.

CAVEAT EMPTOR - Let the buyer beware. This term expresses the rule that the purchaser of an article must examine, judge, and test it for himself, being bound to discover any obvious defects or imperfections.

CERTIFICATE - A written representation that some legal formality has been complied with.

CERTIORARI - To be informed of; the name of a writ issued by a superior court directing the lower court to send up to the former the record and proceedings of a case.

CHANGE OF VENUE - To remove place of trial from one place to another.

CHARGE - An obligation or duty; a formal complaint; an instruction of the court to the jury upon a case.

CHARTER - (n.) The authority by virtue of which an organized body acts;
    (v.) in mercantile law, it means to hire or lease a vehicle or vessel for transportation.

CHATTEL - An article of personal property.

CHATTEL MORTGAGE - A mortgage on personal property.

CIRCUIT - A division of the country, for the administration of justice; a geographical area served by a court.

CITATION - The act of the court by which a person is summoned or cited; also, a reference to legal authority.

CIVIL (ACTIONS)- It indicates the private rights and remedies of individuals in contrast to the word "criminal" (actions) which relates to prosecution for violation of laws.

CLAIM (n.) - Any demand held or asserted as of right.

CODICIL - An addition to a will.

CODIFY - To arrange the laws of a country into a code.

COGNIZANCE - Notice or knowledge.

COLLATERAL - By the side; accompanying; an article or thing given to secure performance of a promise.

COMITY - Courtesy; the practice by which one court follows the decision of another court on the same question.

COMMIT - To perform, as an act; to perpetrate, as a crime; to send a person to prison.

COMMON LAW - As distinguished from law created by the enactment of the legislature (called statutory law), it relates to those principles and rules of action which derive their authority solely from usages and customs of immemorial antiquity, particularly with reference to the ancient unwritten law of England. The written pronouncements of the common law are found in court decisions.

COMMUTE - Change punishment to one less severe.

COMPLAINANT - One who applies to the court for legal redress.
COMPLAINT - The pleading of a plaintiff in a civil action; or a charge that a person has committed a specified offense.
COMPROMISE - An arrangement for settling a dispute by agreement.
CONCUR - To agree, consent.
CONCURRENT - Running together, at the same time.
CONDEMNATION - Taking private property for public use on payment therefor.
CONDITION - Mode or state of being; a qualification or restriction.
CONDUCT - Active and passive behavior; both verbal and nonverbal.
CONFESSION - Voluntary statement of guilt of crime.
CONFIDENTIAL COMMUNICATION BETWEEN CLIENT AND LAWYER - Information transmitted between a client and his lawyer in the course of that relationship and in confidence by a means which, so far as the client is aware, discloses the information to no third persons other than those who are present to further the interest of the client in the consultation or those to whom disclosure is reasonably necessary for the transmission of the information or the accomplishment of the purpose for which the lawyer is consulted, and includes a legal opinion formed and the advice given by the lawyer in the course of that relationship.
CONFRONTATION - Witness testifying in presence of defendant.
CONSANGUINITY - Blood relationship.
CONSIGN - To give in charge; commit; entrust; to send or transmit goods to a merchant, factor, or agent for sale.
CONSIGNEE - One to whom a consignment is made.
CONSIGNOR - One who sends or makes a consignment.
CONSPIRACY - In criminal law, it means an agreement between two or more persons to commit an unlawful act.
CONSPIRATORS - Persons involved in a conspiracy.
CONSTITUTION - The fundamental law of a nation or state.
CONSTRUCTION OF GENDERS - The masculine gender includes the feminine and neuter.
CONSTRUCTION OF SINGULAR AND PLURAL - The singular number includes the plural; and the plural, the singular.
CONSTRUCTION OF TENSES - The present tense includes the past and future tenses; and the future, the present.
CONSTRUCTIVE - An act or condition assumed from other parts or conditions.
CONSTRUE - To ascertain the meaning of language.
CONSUMMATE - To complete.
CONTIGUOUS - Adjoining; touching; bounded by.
CONTINGENT - Possible, but not assured; dependent upon some condition.
CONTINUANCE - The adjournment or postponement of an action pending in a court.
CONTRA - Against, opposed to; contrary.
CONTRACT - An agreement between two or more persons to do or not to do a particular thing.
CONTROVERT - To dispute, deny.
CONVERSION - Dealing with the personal property of another as if it were one's own, without right.
CONVEYANCE - An instrument transferring title to land.
CONVICTION - Generally, the result of a criminal trial which ends in a judgment or sentence that the defendant is guilty as charged.

COOPERATIVE - A cooperative is a voluntary organization of persons with a common interest, formed and operated along democratic lines for the purpose of supplying services at cost to its members and other patrons, who contribute both capital and business.
CORPUS DELICTI - The body of a crime; the crime itself.
CORROBORATE - To strengthen; to add weight by additional evidence.
COUNTERCLAIM - A claim presented by a defendant in opposition to or deduction from the claim of the plaintiff.
COUNTY - Political subdivision of a state.
COVENANT - Agreement.
CREDIBLE - Worthy of belief.
CREDITOR - A person to whom a debt is owing by another person, called the "debtor."
CRIMINAL ACTION - Includes criminal proceedings.
CRIMINAL INFORMATION - Same as complaint.
CRITERION (sing.)
CRITERIA (plural) - A means or tests for judging; a standard or standards.
CROSS-EXAMINATION - Examination of a witness by a party other than the direct examiner upon a matter that is within the scope of the direct examination of the witness.
CULPABLE - Blamable.
CY-PRES - As near as (possible). The rule of *cy-pres* is a rule for the construction of instruments in equity by which the intention of the party is carried out *as near as may be*, when it would be impossible or illegal to give it literal effect.

D

DAMAGES - A monetary compensation, which may be recovered in the courts by any person who has suffered loss, or injury, whether to his person, property or rights through the unlawful act or omission or negligence of another.
DECLARANT - A person who makes a statement.
DE FACTO - In fact; actually but without legal authority.
DE JURE - Of right; legitimate; lawful.
DE MINIMIS - Very small or trifling.
DE NOVO - Anew; afresh; a second time.
DEBT - A specified sum of money owing to one person from another, including not only the obligation of the debtor to pay, but the right of the creditor to receive and enforce payment.
DECEDENT - A dead person.
DECISION - A judgment or decree pronounced by a court in determination of a case.
DECREE - An order of the court, determining the rights of all parties to a suit.
DEED - A writing containing a contract sealed and delivered; particularly to convey real property.
DEFALCATION - Misappropriation of funds.
DEFAMATION - Injuring one's reputation by false statements.
DEFAULT - The failure to fulfill a duty, observe a promise, discharge an obligation, or perform an agreement.
DEFENDANT - The person defending or denying; the party against whom relief or recovery is sought in an action or suit.
DEFRAUD - To practice fraud; to cheat or trick.
DELEGATE (v.)- To entrust to the care or management of another.
DELICTUS - A crime.
DEMUR (v.) - To dispute the sufficiency in law of the pleading of the other side.

DEMURRAGE - In maritime law, it means, the sum fixed or allowed as remuneration to the owners of a ship for the detention of their vessel beyond the number of days allowed for loading and unloading or for sailing; also used in railroad terminology.
DENIAL - A form of pleading; refusing to admit the truth of a statement, charge, etc.
DEPONENT - One who gives testimony under oath reduced to writing.
DEPOSITION - Testimony given under oath outside of court for use in court or for the purpose of obtaining information in preparation for trial of a case.
DETERIORATION - A degeneration such as from decay, corrosion or disintegration.
DETRIMENT - Any loss or harm to person or property.
DEVIATION - A turning aside.
DEVISE - A gift of real property by the last will and testament of the donor.
DICTUM (sing.)
DICTA (plural) - Any statements made by the court in an opinion concerning some rule of law not necessarily involved nor essential to the determination of the case.
DIRECT EVIDENCE - Evidence that directly proves a fact, without an inference or presumption, and which in itself if true, conclusively establishes that fact.
DIRECT EXAMINATION - The first examination of a witness upon a matter that is not within the scope of a previous examination of the witness.
DISAFFIRM - To repudiate.
DISMISS - In an action or suit, it means to dispose of the case without any further consideration or hearing.
DISSENT - To denote disagreement of one or more judges of a court with the decision passed by the majority upon a case before them.
DOCKET (n.) - A formal record, entered in brief, of the proceedings in a court.
DOCTRINE - A rule, principle, theory of law.
DOMICILE - That place where a man has his true, fixed and permanent home to which whenever he is absent he has the intention of returning.
DRAFT (n.) - A commercial paper ordering payment of money drawn by one person on another.
DRAWEE - The person who is requested to pay the money.
DRAWER - The person who draws the commercial paper and addresses it to the drawee.
DUPLICATE - A counterpart produced by the same impression as the original enlargements and miniatures, or by mechanical or electronic re-recording, or by chemical reproduction, or by other equivalent technique which accurately reproduces the original.
DURESS - Use of force to compel performance or non-performance of an act.

E

EASEMENT - A liberty, privilege, or advantage without profit, in the lands of another.
EGRESS - Act or right of going out or leaving; emergence.
EIUSDEM GENERIS - Of the same kind, class or nature. A rule used in the construction of language in a legal document.
EMBEZZLEMENT - To steal; to appropriate fraudulently to one's own use property entrusted to one's care.
EMBRACERY - Unlawful attempt to influence jurors, etc., but not by offering value.
EMINENT DOMAIN - The right of a state to take private property for public use.
ENACT - To make into a law.
ENDORSEMENT - Act of writing one's name on the back of a note, bill or similar written instrument.

ENJOIN - To require a person, by writ of injunction from a court of equity, to perform or to abstain or desist from some act.
ENTIRETY - The whole; that which the law considers as one whole, and not capable of being divided into parts.
ENTRAPMENT - Inducing one to commit a crime so as to arrest him.
ENUMERATED - Mentioned specifically; designated.
ENURE - To operate or take effect.
EQUITY - In its broadest sense, this term denotes the spirit and the habit of fairness, justness, and right dealing which regulate the conduct of men.
ERROR - A mistake of law, or the false or irregular application of law as will nullify the judicial proceedings.
ESCROW - A deed, bond or other written engagement, delivered to a third person, to be delivered by him only upon the performance or fulfillment of some condition.
ESTATE - The interest which any one has in lands, or in any other subject of property.
ESTOP - To stop, bar, or impede.
ESTOPPEL - A rule of law which prevents a man from alleging or denying a fact, because of his own previous act.
ET AL. (alii) - And others.
ET SEQ. (sequential) - And the following.
ET UX. (uxor) - And wife.
EVIDENCE - Testimony, writings, material objects, or other things presented to the senses that are offered to prove the existence or non-existence of a fact.
   Means from which inferences may be drawn as a basis of proof in duly constituted judicial or fact finding tribunals, and includes testimony in the form of opinion and hearsay.
EX CONTRACTU
EX DELICTO - In law, rights and causes of action are divided into two classes, those arising *ex contractu* (from a contract) and those arising *ex delicto* (from a delict or tort).
EX OFFICIO - From office; by virtue of the office.
EX PARTE - On one side only; by or for one.
EX POST FACTO - After the fact.
EX POST FACTO LAW - A law passed after an act was done which retroactively makes such act a crime.
EX REL. (relations) - Upon relation or information.
EXCEPTION - An objection upon a matter of law to a decision made, either before or after judgment by a court.
EXECUTOR (male)
EXECUTRIX (female) - A person who has been appointed by will to execute the will.
EXECUTORY - That which is yet to be executed or performed.
EXEMPT - To release from some liability to which others are subject.
EXONERATION - The removal of a burden, charge or duty.
EXTRADITION - Surrender of a fugitive from one nation to another.

F

F.A.S.- "Free alongside ship"; delivery at dock for ship named.
F.O.B.- "Free on board"; seller will deliver to car, truck, vessel, or other conveyance by which goods are to be transported, without expense or risk of loss to the buyer or consignee.
FABRICATE - To construct; to invent a false story.
FACSIMILE - An exact or accurate copy of an original instrument.

FACTOR - A commercial agent.
FEASANCE - The doing of an act.
FELONIOUS - Criminal, malicious.
FELONY - Generally, a criminal offense that may be punished by death or imprisonment for more than one year as differentiated from a misdemeanor.
FEME SOLE - A single woman.
FIDUCIARY - A person who is invested with rights and powers to be exercised for the benefit of another person.
FIERI FACIAS - A writ of execution commanding the sheriff to levy and collect the amount of a judgment from the goods and chattels of the judgment debtor.
FINDING OF FACT - Determination from proof or judicial notice of the existence of a fact. A ruling implies a supporting finding of fact; no separate or formal finding is required unless required by a statute of this state.
FISCAL - Relating to accounts or the management of revenue.
FORECLOSURE (sale) - A sale of mortgaged property to obtain satisfaction of the mortgage out of the sale proceeds.
FORFEITURE - A penalty, a fine.
FORGERY - Fabricating or producing falsely, counterfeited.
FORTUITOUS - Accidental.
FORUM - A court of justice; a place of jurisdiction.
FRAUD - Deception; trickery.
FREEHOLDER - One who owns real property.
FUNGIBLE - Of such kind or nature that one specimen or part may be used in the place of another.

G

GARNISHEE - Person garnished.
GARNISHMENT - A legal process to reach the money or effects of a defendant, in the possession or control of a third person.
GRAND JURY - Not less than 16, not more than 23 citizens of a county sworn to inquire into crimes committed or triable in the county.
GRANT - To agree to; convey, especially real property.
GRANTEE - The person to whom a grant is made.
GRANTOR - The person by whom a grant is made.
GRATUITOUS - Given without a return, compensation or consideration.
GRAVAMEN - The grievance complained of or the substantial cause of a criminal action.
GUARANTY (n.) - A promise to answer for the payment of some debt, or the performance of some duty, in case of the failure of another person, who, in the first instance, is liable for such payment or performance.
GUARDIAN - The person, committee, or other representative authorized by law to protect the person or estate or both of an incompetent (or of a *sui juris* person having a guardian) and to act for him in matters affecting his person or property or both. An incompetent is a person under disability imposed by law.
GUILTY - Establishment of the fact that one has committed a breach of conduct; especially, a violation of law.

H

HABEAS CORPUS - You have the body; the name given to a variety of writs, having for their object to bring a party before a court or judge for decision as to whether such person is being lawfully held prisoner.
HABENDUM - In conveyancing; it is the clause in a deed conveying land which defines the extent of ownership to be held by the grantee.
HEARING - A proceeding whereby the arguments of the interested parties are heared.
HEARSAY - A type of testimony given by a witness who relates, not what he knows personally, but what others have told hi, or what he has heard said by others.
HEARSAY RULE, THE - (a) "Hearsay evidence" is evidence of a statement that was made other than by a witness while testifying at the hearing and that is offered to prove the truth of the matter stated; (b) Except as provided by law, hearsay evidence is inadmissible; (c) This section shall be known and may be cited as the hearsay rule.
HEIR - Generally, one who inherits property, real or personal.
HOLDER OF THE PRIVILEGE - (a) The client when he has no guardian or conservator; (b) A guardian or conservator of the client when the client has a guardian or conservator; (c) The personal representative of the client if the client is dead; (d) A successor, assign, trustee in dissolution, or any similar representative of a firm, association, organization, partnership, business trust, corporation, or public entity that is no longer in existence.
HUNG JURY - One so divided that they can't agree on a verdict.
HUSBAND-WIFE PRIVILEGE - An accused in a criminal proceeding has a privilege to prevent his spouse from testifying against him.
HYPOTHECATE - To pledge a thing without delivering it to the pledgee.
HYPOTHESIS - A supposition, assumption, or toehry.

I

I.E. (id est) - That is.
IB., OR IBID.(ibidem) - In the same place; used to refer to a legal reference previously cited to avoid repeating the entire citation.
ILLICIT - Prohibited; unlawful.
ILLUSORY - Deceiving by false appearance.
IMMUNITY - Exemption.
IMPEACH - To accuse, to dispute.
IMPEDIMENTS - Disabilities, or hindrances.
IMPLEAD - To sue or prosecute by due course of law.
IMPUTED - Attributed or charged to.
IN LOCO PARENTIS - In place of parent, a guardian.
IN TOTO - In the whole; completely.
INCHOATE - Imperfect; unfinished.
INCOMMUNICADO - Denial of the right of a prisoner to communicate with friends or relatives.
INCOMPETENT - One who is incapable of caring for his own affairs because he is mentally deficient or undeveloped.
INCRIMINATION - A matter will incriminate a person if it constitutes, or forms an essential part of, or, taken in connection with other matters disclosed, is a basis for a reasonable inference of such a violation of the laws of this State as to subject him to liability to punishment therefor, unless he has become for any reason permanently immune from punishment for such violation.
INCUMBRANCE - Generally a claim, lien, charge or liability attached to and binding real property.

INDEMNIFY - To secure against loss or damage; also, to make reimbursement to one for a loss already incurred by him.
INDEMNITY - An agreement to reimburse another person in case of an anticipated loss falling upon him.
INDICIA - Signs; indications.
INDICTMENT - An accusation in writing found and presented by a grand jury charging that a person has committed a crime.
INDORSE - To write a name on the back of a legal paper or document, generally, a negotiable instrument
INDUCEMENT - Cause or reason why a thing is done or that which incites the person to do the act or commit a crime; the motive for the criminal act.
INFANT - In civil cases one under 21 years of age.
INFORMATION - A formal accusation of crime made by a prosecuting attorney.
INFRA - Below, under; this word occurring by itself in a publication refers the reader to a future part of the publication.
INGRESS - The act of going into.
INJUNCTION - A writ or order by the court requiring a person, generally, to do or to refrain from doing an act.
INSOLVENT - The condition of a person who is unable to pay his debts.
INSTRUCTION - A direction given by the judge to the jury concerning the law of the case.
INTERIM - In the meantime; time intervening.
INTERLOCUTORY - Temporary, not final; something intervening between the commencement and the end of a suit which decides some point or matter, but is not a final decision of the whole controversy.
INTERROGATORIES - A series of formal written questions used in the examination of a party or a witness usually prior to a trial.
INTESTATE - A person who dies without a will.
INURE - To result, to take effect.
IPSO FACTO - By the fact iself; by the mere fact.
ISSUE (n.) The disputed point or question in a case,

J

JEOPARDY - Danger, hazard, peril.
JOINDER - Joining; uniting with another person in some legal steps or proceeding.
JOINT - United; combined.
JUDGE - Member or members or representative or representatives of a court conducting a trial or hearing at which evidence is introduced.
JUDGMENT - The official decision of a court of justice.
JUDICIAL OR JUDICIARY - Relating to or connected with the administration of justice.
JURAT - The clause written at the foot of an affidavit, stating when, where and before whom such affidavit was sworn.
JURISDICTION - The authority to hear and determine controversies between parties.
JURISPRUDENCE - The philosophy of law.
JURY - A body of persons legally selected to inquire into any matter of fact, and to render their verdict according to the evidence.

L

LACHES - The failure to diligently assert a right, which results in a refusal to allow relief.

LANDLORD AND TENANT - A phrase used to denote the legal relation existing between the owner and occupant of real estate.

LARCENY - Stealing personal property belonging to another.

LATENT - Hidden; that which does not appear on the face of a thing.

LAW - Includes constitutional, statutory, and decisional law.

LAWYER-CLIENT PRIVILEGE - (1) A "client" is a person, public officer, or corporation, association, or other organization or entity, either public or private, who is rendered professional legal services by a lawyer, or who consults a lawyer with a view to obtaining professional legal services from him; (2) A "lawyer" is a person authorized, or reasonably believed by the client to be authorized, to practice law in any state or nation; (3) A "representative of the lawyer" is one employed to assist the lawyer in the rendition of professional legal services; (4) A communication is "confidential" if not intended to be disclosed to third persons other than those to whom disclosure is in furtherance of the rendition of professional legal services to the client or those reasonably necessary for the transmission of the communication.

General rule of privilege - A client has a privilege to refuse to disclose and to prevent any other person from disclosing confidential communications made for the purpose of facilitating the rendition of professional legal services to the client, (1) between himself or his representative and his lawyer or his lawyer's representative, or (2) between his lawyer and the lawyer's representative, or (3) by him or his lawyer to a lawyer representing another in a matter of common interest, or (4) between representatives of the client or between the client and a representative of the client, or (5) between lawyers representing the client.

LEADING QUESTION - Question that suggests to the witness the answer that the examining party desires.

LEASE - A contract by which one conveys real estate for a limited time usually for a specified rent; personal property also may be leased.

LEGISLATION - The act of enacting laws.

LEGITIMATE - Lawful.

LESSEE - One to whom a lease is given.

LESSOR - One who grants a lease

LEVY - A collecting or exacting by authority.

LIABLE - Responsible; bound or obligated in law or equity.

LIBEL (v.) - To defame or injure a person's reputation by a published writing.

(n.) - The initial pleading on the part of the plaintiff in an admiralty proceeding.

LIEN - A hold or claim which one person has upon the property of another as a security for some debt or charge.

LIQUIDATED - Fixed; settled.

LIS PENDENS - A pending civil or criminal action.

LITERAL - According to the language.

LITIGANT - A party to a lawsuit.

LITATION - A judicial controversy.

LOCUS - A place.

LOCUS DELICTI - Place of the crime.

LOCUS POENITENTIAE - The abandoning or giving up of one's intention to commit some crime before it is fully completed or abandoning a conspiracy before its purpose is accomplished.

M

MALFEASANCE - To do a wrongful act.

MALICE - The doing of a wrongful act Intentionally without just cause or excuse.

MANDAMUS - The name of a writ issued by a court to enforce the performance of some public duty.
MANDATORY (adj.) Containing a command.
MARITIME - Pertaining to the sea or to commerce thereon.
MARSHALING - Arranging or disposing of in order.
MAXIM - An established principle or proposition.
MINISTERIAL - That which involves obedience to instruction, but demands no special discretion, judgment or skill.
MISAPPROPRIATE - Dealing fraudulently with property entrusted to one.
MISDEMEANOR - A crime less than a felony and punishable by a fine or imprisonment for less than one year.
MISFEASANCE - Improper performance of a lawful act.
MISREPRESENTATION - An untrue representation of facts.
MITIGATE - To make or become less severe, harsh.
MITTIMUS - A warrant of commitment to prison.
MOOT (adj.) Unsettled, undecided, not necessary to be decided.
MORTGAGE - A conveyance of property upon condition, as security for the payment of a debt or the performance of a duty, and to become void upon payment or performance according to the stipulated terms.
MORTGAGEE - A person to whom property is mortgaged.
MORTGAGOR - One who gives a mortgage.
MOTION - In legal proceedings, a "motion" is an application, either written or oral, addressed to the court by a party to an action or a suit requesting the ruling of the court on a matter of law.
MUTUALITY - Reciprocation.

N

NEGLIGENCE - The failure to exercise that degree of care which an ordinarily prudent person would exercise under like circumstances.
NEGOTIABLE (instrument) - Any instrument obligating the payment of money which is transferable from one person to another by endorsement and delivery or by delivery only.
NEGOTIATE - To transact business; to transfer a negotiable instrument; to seek agreement for the amicable disposition of a controversy or case.
NOLLE PROSEQUI - A formal entry upon the record, by the plaintiff in a civil suit or the prosecuting officer in a criminal action, by which he declares that he "will no further prosecute" the case.
NOLO CONTENDERE - The name of a plea in a criminal action, having the same effect as a plea of guilty; but not constituting a direct admission of guilt.
NOMINAL - Not real or substantial.
NOMINAL DAMAGES - Award of a trifling sum where no substantial injury is proved to have been sustained.
NONFEASANCE - Neglect of duty.
NOVATION - The substitution of a new debt or obligation for an existing one.
NUNC PRO TUNC - A phrase applied to acts allowed to be done after the time when they should be done, with a retroactive effect.("Now for then.")

O

OATH - Oath includes affirmation or declaration under penalty of perjury.
OBITER DICTUM - Opinion expressed by a court on a matter not essentially involved in a case and hence not a decision; also called dicta, if plural.

OBJECT (v.) - To oppose as improper or illegal and referring the question of its propriety or legality to the court.
OBLIGATION - A legal duty, by which a person is bound to do or not to do a certain thing.
OBLIGEE - The person to whom an obligation is owed.
OBLIGOR - The person who is to perform the obligation.
OFFER (v.) - To present for acceptance or rejection.
 (n.) - A proposal to do a thing, usually a proposal to make a contract.
OFFICIAL INFORMATION - Information within the custody or control of a department or agency of the government the disclosure of which is shown to be contrary to the public interest.
OFFSET - A deduction.
ONUS PROBANDI - Burden of proof.
OPINION - The statement by a judge of the decision reached in a case, giving the law as applied to the case and giving reasons for the judgment; also a belief or view.
OPTION - The exercise of the power of choice; also a privilege existing in one person, for which he has paid money, which gives him the right to buy or sell real or personal property at a given price within a specified time.
ORDER - A rule or regulation; every direction of a court or judge made or entered in writing but not including a judgment.
ORDINANCE - Generally, a rule established by authority; also commonly used to designate the legislative acts of a municipal corporation.
ORIGINAL - Writing or recording itself or any counterpart intended to have the same effect by a person executing or issuing it. An "original" of a photograph includes the negative or any print therefrom. If data are stored in a computer or similar device, any printout or other output readable by sight, shown to reflect the data accurately, is an "original."
OVERT - Open, manifest.

P

PANEL - A group of jurors selected to serve during a term of the court.
PARENS PATRIAE - Sovereign power of a state to protect or be a guardian over children and incompetents.
PAROL - Oral or verbal.
PAROLE - To release one in prison before the expiration of his sentence, conditionally.
PARITY - Equality in purchasing power between the farmer and other segments of the economy.
PARTITION - A legal division of real or personal property between one or more owners.
PARTNERSHIP - An association of two or more persons to carry on as co-owners a business for profit.
PATENT (adj.) - Evident.
 (n.) - A grant of some privilege, property, or authority, made by the government or sovereign of a country to one or more individuals.
PECULATION - Stealing.
PECUNIARY - Monetary.
PENULTIMATE - Next to the last.
PER CURIAM - A phrase used in the report of a decision to distinguish an opinion of the whole court from an opinion written by any one judge.
PER SE - In itself; taken alone.
PERCEIVE - To acquire knowledge through one's senses.
PEREMPTORY - Imperative; absolute.
PERJURY - To lie or state falsely under oath.

PERPETUITY - Perpetual existence; also the quality or condition of an estate limited so that it will not take effect or vest within the period fixed by law.
PERSON - Includes a natural person, firm, association, organization, partnership, business trust, corporation, or public entity.
PERSONAL PROPERTY - Includes money, goods, chattels, things in action, and evidences of debt.
PERSONALTY - Short term for personal property.
PETITION - An application in writing for an order of the court, stating the circumstances upon which it is founded and requesting any order or other relief from a court.
PLAINTIFF - A person who brings a court action.
PLEA - A pleading in a suit or action.
PLEADINGS - Formal allegations made by the parties of their respective claims and defenses, for the judgment of the court.
PLEDGE - A deposit of personal property as a security for the performance of an act.
PLEDGEE - The party to whom goods are delivered in pledge.
PLEDGOR - The party delivering goods in pledge.
PLENARY - Full; complete.
POLICE POWER - Inherent power of the state or its political subdivisions to enact laws within constitutional limits to promote the general welfare of society or the community.
POLLING THE JURY - Call the names of persons on a jury and requiring each juror to declare what his verdict is before it is legally recorded.
POST MORTEM - After death.
POWER OF ATTORNEY - A writing authorizing one to act for another.
PRECEPT - An order, warrant, or writ issued to an officer or body of officers, commanding him or them to do some act within the scope of his or their powers.
PRELIMINARY FACT - Fact upon the existence or nonexistence of which depends the admissibility or inadmissibility of evidence. The phrase "the admissibility or inadmissibility of evidence" includes the qualification or disqualification of a person to be a witness and the existence or nonexistence of a privilege.
PREPONDERANCE - Outweighing.
PRESENTMENT - A report by a grand jury on something they have investigated on their own knowledge.
PRESUMPTION - An assumption of fact resulting from a rule of law which requires such fact to be assumed from another fact or group of facts found or otherwise established in the action.
PRIMA FACUE - At first sight.
PRIMA FACIE CASE - A case where the evidence is very patent against the defendant.
PRINCIPAL - The source of authority or rights; a person primarily liable as differentiated from "principle" as a primary or basic doctrine.
PRO AND CON - For and against.
PRO RATA - Proportionally.
PROBATE - Relating to proof, especially to the proof of wills.
PROBATIVE - Tending to prove.
PROCEDURE - In law, this term generally denotes rules which are established by the Federal, State, or local Governments regarding the types of pleading and courtroom practice which must be followed by the parties involved in a criminal or civil case.
PROCLAMATION - A public notice by an official of some order, intended action, or state of facts.

PROFFERED EVIDENCE - The admissibility or inadmissibility of which is dependent upon the existence or nonexistence of a preliminary fact.
PROMISSORY (NOTE) - A promise in writing to pay a specified sum at an expressed time, or on demand, or at sight, to a named person, or to his order, or bearer.
PROOF - The establishment by evidence of a requisite degree of belief concerning a fact in the mind of the trier of fact or the court.
PROPERTY - Includes both real and personal property.
PROPRIETARY (adj.) - Relating or pertaining to ownership; usually a single owner.
PROSECUTE - To carry on an action or other judicial proceeding; to proceed against a person criminally.
PROVISO - A limitation or condition in a legal instrument.
PROXIMATE - Immediate; nearest
PUBLIC EMPLOYEE - An officer, agent, or employee of a public entity.
PUBLIC ENTITY - Includes a national, state, county, city and county, city, district, public authority, public agency, or any other political subdivision or public corporation, whether foreign or domestic.
PUBLIC OFFICIAL - Includes an official of a political dubdivision of such state or territory and of a municipality.
PUNITIVE - Relating to punishment.

Q

QUASH - To make void.
QUASI - As if; as it were.
QUID PRO QUO - Something for something; the giving of one valuable thing for another.
QUITCLAIM (v.) - To release or relinquish claim or title to, especially in deeds to realty.
QUO WARRANTO - A legal procedure to test an official's right to a public office or the right to hold a franchise, or to hold an office in a domestic corporation.

R

RATIFY - To approve and sanction.
REAL PROPERTY - Includes lands, tenements, and hereditaments.
REALTY - A brief term for real property.
REBUT - To contradict; to refute, especially by evidence and arguments.
RECEIVER - A person who is appointed by the court to receive, and hold in trust property in litigation.
RECIDIVIST - Habitual criminal.
RECIPROCAL - Mutual.
RECOUPMENT - To keep back or get something which is due; also, it is the right of a defendant to have a deduction from the amount of the plaintiff's damages because the plaintiff has not fulfilled his part of the same contract.
RECROSS EXAMINATION - Examination of a witness by a cross-examiner subsequent to a redirect examination of the witness.
REDEEM - To release an estate or article from mortgage or pledge by paying the debt for which it stood as security.
REDIRECT EXAMINATION - Examination of a witness by the direct examiner subsequent to the cross-examination of the witness.
REFEREE - A person to whom a cause pending in a court is referred by the court, to take testimony, hear the parties, and report thereon to the court.

REFERENDUM - A method of submitting an important legislative or administrative matter to a direct vote of the people.
RELEVANT EVIDENCE - Evidence including evidence relevant to the credulity of a witness or hearsay declarant, having any tendency in reason to prove or disprove any disputed fact that is of consequence to the determination of the action.
REMAND - To send a case back to the lower court from which it came, for further proceedings.
REPLEVIN - An action to recover goods or chattels wrongfully taken or detained.
REPLY (REPLICATION) - Generally, a reply is what the plaintiff or other person who has instituted proceedings says in answer to the defendant's case.
RE JUDICATA - A thing judicially acted upon or decided.
RES ADJUDICATA - Doctrine that an issue or dispute litigated and determined in a case between the opposing parties is deemed permanently decided between these parties.
RESCIND (RECISSION) - To avoid or cancel a contract.
RESPONDENT - A defendant in a proceeding in chancery or admiralty; also, the person who contends against the appeal in a case.
RESTITUTION - In equity, it is the restoration of both parties to their original condition (when practicable), upon the rescission of a contract for fraud or similar cause.
RETROACTIVE (RETROSPECTIVE) - Looking back; effective as of a prior time.
REVERSED - A term used by appellate courts to indicate that the decision of the lower court in the case before it has been set aside.
REVOKE - To recall or cancel.
RIPARIAN (RIGHTS) - The rights of a person owning land containing or bordering on a water course or other body of water, such as lakes and rivers.

S

SALE - A contract whereby the ownership of property is transferred from one person to another for a sum of money or for any consideration.
SANCTION - A penalty or punishment provided as a means of enforcing obedience to a law; also, an authorization.
SATISFACTION - The discharge of an obligation by paying a party what is due to him; or what is awarded to him by the judgment of a court or otherwise.
SCIENTER - Knowingly; also, it is used in pleading to denote the defendant's guilty knowledge.
SCINTILLA - A spark; also the least particle.
SECRET OF STATE - Governmental secret relating to the national defense or the international relations of the United States.
SECURITY - Indemnification; the term is applied to an obligation, such as a mortgage or deed of trust, given by a debtor to insure the payment or performance of his debt, by furnishing the creditor with a resource to be used in case of the debtor's failure to fulfill the principal obligation.
SENTENCE - The judgment formally pronounced by the court or judge upon the defendant after his conviction in a criminal prosecution.
SET-OFF - A claim or demand which one party in an action credits against the claim of the opposing party.
SHALL and MAY - "Shall" is mandatory and "may" is permissive.
SITUS - Location.
SOVEREIGN - A person, body or state in which independent and supreme authority is vested.
STARE DECISIS - To follow decided cases.

STATE - "State" means this State, unless applied to the different parts of the United States. In the latter case, it includes any state, district, commonwealth, territory or insular possession of the United States, including the District of Columbia.

STATEMENT - (a) Oral or written verbal expression or (b) nonverbal conduct of a person intended by him as a substitute for oral or written verbal expression.

STATUTE - An act of the legislature. Includes a treaty.

STATUTE OF LIMITATION - A statute limiting the time to bring an action after the right of action has arisen.

STAY - To hold in abeyance an order of a court.

STIPULATION - Any agreement made by opposing attorneys regulating any matter incidental to the proceedings or trial.

SUBORDINATION (AGREEMENT) - An agreement making one's rights inferior to or of a lower rank than another's.

SUBORNATION - The crime of procuring a person to lie or to make false statements to a court.

SUBPOENA - A writ or order directed to a person, and requiring his attendance at a particular time and place to testify as a witness.

SUBPOENA DUCES TECUM - A subpoena used, not only for the purpose of compelling witnesses to attend in court, but also requiring them to bring with them books or documents which may be in their possession, and which may tend to elucidate the subject matter of the trial.

SUBROGATION - The substituting of one for another as a creditor, the new creditor succeeding to the former's rights.

SUBSIDY - A government grant to assist a private enterprise deemed advantageous to the public.

SUI GENERIS - Of the same kind.

SUIT - Any civil proceeding by a person or persons against another or others in a court of justice by which the plaintiff pursues the remedies afforded him by law.

SUMMONS - A notice to a defendant that an action against him has been commenced and requiring him to appear in court and answer the complaint.

SUPRA - Above; this word occurring by itself in a book refers the reader to a previous part of the book.

SURETY - A person who binds himself for the payment of a sum of money, or for the performance of something else, for another.

SURPLUSAGE - Extraneous or unnecessary matter.

SURVIVORSHIP - A term used when a person becomes entitled to property by reason of his having survived another person who had an interest in the property.

SUSPEND SENTENCE - Hold back a sentence pending good behavior of prisoner.

SYLLABUS - A note prefixed to a report, especially a case, giving a brief statement of the court's ruling on different issues of the case.

T

TALESMAN - Person summoned to fill a panel of jurors.

TENANT - One who holds or possesses lands by any kind of right or title; also, one who has the temporary use and occupation of real property owned by another person (landlord), the duration and terms of his tenancy being usually fixed by an instrument called "a lease."

TENDER - An offer of money; an expression of willingness to perform a contract according to its terms.

TERM - When used with reference to a court, it signifies the period of time during which the court holds a session, usually of several weeks or months duration.

TESTAMENTARY - Pertaining to a will or the administration of a will.
TESTATOR (male)
TESTATRIX (female) - One who makes or has made a testament or will.
TESTIFY (TESTIMONY) - To give evidence under oath as a witness.
TO WIT - That is to say; namely.
TORT - Wrong; injury to the person.
TRANSITORY - Passing from place to place.
TRESPASS - Entry into another's ground, illegally.
TRIAL - The examination of a cause, civil or criminal, before a judge who has jurisdiction over it, according to the laws of the land.
TRIER OF FACT - Includes (a) the jury and (b) the court when the court is trying an issue of fact other than one relating to the admissibility of evidence.
TRUST - A right of property, real or personal, held by one party for the benefit of another.
TRUSTEE - One who lawfully holds property in custody for the benefit of another.

U

UNAVAILABLE AS A WITNESS - The declarant is (1) Exempted or precluded on the ground of privilege from testifying concerning the matter to which his statement is relevant; (2) Disqualified from testifying to the matter; (3) Dead or unable to attend or to testify at the hearing because of then existing physical or mental illness or infirmity; (4) Absent from the hearing and the court is unable to compel his attendance by its process; or (5) Absent from the hearing and the proponent of his statement has exercised reasonable diligence but has been unable to procure his attendance by the court's process.
ULTRA VIRES - Acts beyond the scope and power of a corporation, association, etc.
UNILATERAL - One-sided; obligation upon, or act of one party.
USURY - Unlawful interest on a loan.

V

VACATE - To set aside; to move out.
VARIANCE - A discrepancy or disagreement between two instruments or two aspects of the same case, which by law should be consistent.
VENDEE - A purchaser or buyer.
VENDOR - The person who transfers property by sale, particularly real estate; the term "seller" is used more commonly for one who sells personal property.
VENIREMEN - Persons ordered to appear to serve on a jury or composing a panel of jurors.
VENUE - The place at which an action is tried, generally based on locality or judicial district in which an injury occurred or a material fact happened.
VERDICT - The formal decision or finding of a jury.
VERIFY - To confirm or substantiate by oath.
VEST - To accrue to.
VOID - Having no legal force or binding effect.
VOIR DIRE - Preliminary examination of a witness or a juror to test competence, interest, prejudice, etc.

W

WAIVE - To give up a right.
WAIVER - The intentional or voluntary relinquishment of a known right.
WARRANT (WARRANTY) (v.) - To promise that a certain fact or state of facts, in relation to the subject matter, is, or shall be, as it is represented to be.

WARRANT (n.) - A writ issued by a judge, or other competent authority, addressed to a sheriff, or other officer, requiring him to arrest the person therein named, and bring him before the judge or court to answer or be examined regarding the offense with which he is charged.

WRIT - An order or process issued in the name of the sovereign or in the name of a court or judicial officer, commanding the performance or nonperformance of some act.

WRITING - Handwriting, typewriting, printing, photostating, photographing and every other means of recording upon any tangible thing any form of communication or representation, including letters, words, pictures, sounds, or symbols, or combinations thereof.

WRITINGS AND RECORDINGS - Consists of letters, words, or numbers, or their equivalent, set down by handwriting, typewriting, printing, photostating, photographing, magnetic impulse, mechanical or electronic recording, or other form of data compilation.

Y

YEA AND NAY - Yes and no.

YELLOW DOG CONTRACT - A contract by which employer requires employee to sign an instrument promising as condition that he will not join a union during its continuance, and will be discharged if he does join.

Z

ZONING - The division of a city by legislative regulation into districts and the prescription and application in each district of regulations having to do with structural and architectural designs of buildings and of regulations prescribing use to which buildings within designated districts may be put.

www.ingramcontent.com/pod-product-compliance
Lightning Source LLC
Chambersburg PA
CBHW081819300426

44116CB00014B/2414